I Have Asperger's

I Have Asperger's

Erin Clemens

Erin Clemens
2014

First Printing: 2014

ISBN 978-1-304-93112-2

www.ihaveaspergers.webs.com

To my best friend, forever and always, my dog

Sadie

Contents

Acknowledgements

I'd like to thank my family and friends for their love and support, plus a special thanks to my Dad for his help with editing the book.

I couldn't have done it without you.

Foreword

(A message for parents, educators, professionals, et. al.)

Over the past year, I've had the task of editing my daughter Erin's manuscript. I must admit, this turned out to be more challenging than I expected. An editor is expected to be a filter, a polisher, one who will take a rambling thought and make it concise. One who will keep the author grounded and from sounding too opinionated or close-minded. Well, Erin is like many people on the spectrum... when she communicates, you get brutal honesty. Exaggeration and fluffing up a story simply isn't an option for her. There is no sugar-coating, no hidden agenda, nothing misrepresented; she speaks from her heart and you get exactly what she is thinking.

So here was the challenge: You can't really edit that without editing her thought process, and ultimately, her message. Erin's goal with this book is to give you a picture of what life is like through her eyes (and as you will soon discover, her nose, ears, mouth, and sense of touch). To rewrite her thoughts might give you something that would flow better, or have more punch, but at the cost of losing something in the translation. Erin's writing has a voice, and the last thing that I wanted to do is compromise that voice for the sake of grammar or composition. To that end, I really tried to limit my edits to things that were clearly errors (affect vs. effect, sight vs. site, etc.) where such a correction would have no risk of changing the content... and hopefully we caught most of those. But in terms of the message itself, I tried to leave it alone.

So what is this book? That may be best described by what it *isn't.* This book is not a professional's doctorate on behavior, it's not the tabulated results of a study, or a collection of data. This book is not a reference manual. There is no chapter that you can thumb to on diagnosis, or behavior modification, or medication, or services. Instead, it's a raw look into the world of a young woman with Asperger's Syndrome, in the form of a journal that takes you through several years of her life. In this journal she gives you an open door into her triumphs, her disappointments, her frustrations. But in doing this, you get something that you can't get from someone who is NOT on the spectrum. You get her perspective. You get to see her thought process, her reasoning. You get to understand why someone with Asperger's doesn't always laugh at the joke, or laughs when they shouldn't. Why they may rock back and forth, why they get frustrated or distracted in a conversation or overwhelmed in a social situation. Why they seem to be listening and just when you think they understand, they go and do something so far out of left field that you wonder, "Where in the world did *that* come from?"

This book gives you the honest thoughts of someone who is an expert on Asperger's Syndrome, because she lives with it 24 hours a day, every day. You're getting it right from the source. And maybe, just maybe, you might read one of those essays and you'll recognize a behavior or pattern. Maybe you'll have that "aha" moment, and you'll see a topic that relates to your son, daughter, brother, sister, spouse, friend, student, or client. And maybe that insight will help you to understand them a little bit more. Maybe that will allow you to be a little more tolerant, a little more accepting. Maybe that will give you the information you need to make their world a little easier. And if that happens, Erin will have accomplished her goal.

- Rob Clemens (editor and father of the author)

Introduction

Growing up was confusing to me. For my whole life, it felt like no matter how hard I tried I couldn't get things right. People gave me strange looks. They became angry over things which didn't make sense to me. It seemed to me that people were just being nit-picky. I tried to tell them that I was lost, but no one seemed to hear me. In 10th grade, after 15 long, tiring years, I was diagnosed with Asperger's Syndrome. Of course, at that time I didn't know what it was. I shrugged off this "official" diagnosis, because after all, I hadn't changed.

What I wasn't expecting was for people to stop being so mad at me. They began to listen. I studied more about what Asperger's was, and my life began to make sense. Now that people had started listening, I felt maybe I could get across what I had been trying to say before. I made a website, www.ihaveaspergers.webs.com and I started to blog about what my life is like. I realized that people who are not on the Autistic Spectrum think, feel, and live differently. It is my job to teach them about what it's like for me.

This book covers my blog posts from when I first started in 2011 through May of 2013. It also has a feature I call *Looking Back*, where I include my current personal thoughts on posts that I have written. (These thoughts lessen towards the end as less time has passed from the blog posts.) Most of the names are fictitious to protect privacy. I never thought that I would be able to write a book, as it seemed like such a daunting task that required way too much patience (and I don't have a lot of that). Blogging has allowed me to accomplish this in a way that I could manage. Instead of feeling overwhelmed by the required amount of writing and time it would take, I spent a few minutes a day recapping events, or jotting down an answer to a common question I would receive. From poems to personal thoughts, and everything in-between, *I Have Asperger's* gives any reader an inside look into my world.

My name is Erin Clemens. I'm 24 years old, and I want to help others understand what my life is like living with Asperger's Syndrome. My hope is that people can learn from what I have been through, and apply it to what may help someone they know on the spectrum. To me, autism isn't a death sentence. It's just a different lifestyle. The views expressed are my own.

The First Month

Bouncy Balls Are Fun!
March 29, 2011 at 9:02 PM

So today started off with my dog waking me up a little extra early, asking to be fed. (Tsk tsk tsk, I know. She shouldn't be doing that!) Don't worry; she was fed when it was time. But she's not allowed to ask for it. (And I like my beauty sleep!)

I volunteer at my local library, pulling the books from the shelves that people have requested holds on. I was impressively fast today, until I got to the childrens' section, where sign-ups were being held for some event. It was really overwhelming and crowded. I had some help though, and got it all done eventually. And soon it all cleared out, too. There was only one book that I couldn't find! (Out of 51!)

Then it was off to my friend's house. We watched the movie Temple Grandin, and then had some extra time which we spent bouncing balls off a ceiling fan! (Kids, DON'T TRY THIS AT HOME!!!!!!!!!) Note: be sure there is NO WAY anything can break when you do this. (We were fine!) And make sure that the ball you use is lightweight, and not much bigger than half an inch. AND make sure you have a strong fan, set on low! Needless to say, it was really awesome.

I Have Asperger's

Looking Back:
I struggled over whether or not I should include this first blog post in this book. Besides the idea of watching the movie Temple Grandin, what does it have to do with Asperger's? I guess that is why I chose to keep it in. Not only was this my first blog post EVER, but it goes to show that at first, it seems to MANY people that I don't have Asperger's. (I get this a LOT.) In later posts, however, it becomes clear that there is something different about me.

What Time Is It?

March 30, 2011 at 1:43 PM

I have had the same make and model watch for years. (Literally. Since maybe 7th or 8th grade.) I buy the same one every time. I love this watch. It's the only one that is quick and easy to use, and doesn't bother my wrist. Or, at least that's what I thought.

I went to buy a new one the other day, and noticed that the band on it was different this time. I'm thinking "ok, so I'll get used to it soon."

Wrong.

Man, does this thing hurt! I actually had to take it off. So now, my battery is nearly dead in my other watch, and this one hurts to wear. But I synced the time of them perfectly! So the trouble is: do I bring back this watch to get enough money to buy (HOPEFULLY) the same watch somewhere else (where the band may be different and feel better)? OR do I try to break in this new one, and put up with it.

Probably the first option. But I'd better decide soon, because I'm going to art tonight, and I'd save gas money if I brought this thing back while I was out there. But I need a watch for art class! Heck, I need a watch for life!

Looking Back:
I learned that the reason the watch was hurting me was because I had bought it at a different store. (It was like store brand versus name brand.) To this day, I still have that same kind of watch. But don't ever look at the time on it – it's twenty minutes fast! (This was once used as a way to keep me from being late, as it tends to take me about twenty minutes to get myself ready for something. Now I'm just so used to this setting that I get confused if it's the correct time!)

People Driving (And Not Parking!)

March 31, 2011 at 3:38 PM

Here's my advice to all of you drivers out there:

Ok, first, get off the cell phone. And put out the cigarette. You shouldn't be distracted while you're driving.

But when you go to park:

DON'T back in to a parking spot. Seriously, if you want to face forward, take a pull-through spot.

I Have Asperger's

DON'T put on your "hazard" lights and park in the fire lane. It's illegal, and if there's ever a fire in one of those building and someone happens to die because you were "waiting" for someone and the fire truck couldn't park, I'll blame you.

DON'T park in the handicapped spot unless you are actually handicapped, and have a marker to say so. Otherwise, that's just plain rude. And also illegal.

DON'T pretend that you didn't realize your car was straddling the line, taking up two entire parking spots. ON the line is fine. Over the line: take two seconds to give the other space to someone else.

DON'T park in the crossed lined space. This is not a parking spot. If it was, I would have taken it, but instead I parked all the way over 'there'. *points far away*

And above all, please,

DON'T WAIT FOR THAT DRIVER WHO IS LEAVING JUST TO GET A BETTER SPOT!!!!! It holds everyone up, and in the end wastes EVERYONE'S time. Hey, see the parking spot about 3 spaces down? It's empty. Please take it so we can all keep moving.

I Finally Joined Twitter!: @AspergerSadie

April 2, 2011 at 8:58 PM

It feels really weird. I've always been one to shy away from social networking. It's a little overwhelming sometimes. But I finally made a twitter account. If that's what it takes to get more awareness, then I can do twitter. (Besides, I like the blue bird.) And I like my twitter name: AspergerSadie. It's "Asperger's" and "Sadie" combined! (I'm known as Sadie555 everywhere)

The only thing is I still don't feel comfortable signing up for Facebook. Besides, my computer would hate me from all the viruses it would get from there.

So, if you would like to help me, add my website to your Facebook. And follow me on my new Twitter account! @AspergerSadie (What's the @ for anyways?!)

Looking Back:

I have since joined Facebook, and found that it has actually been a great way to connect with the people in the autism community! You can follow me on Facebook at

www.facebook.com/erin.clemens.58

Autism Awareness Month

April 3, 2011 at 12:54 PM

First, YESTERDAY (April 2) was World Autism Awareness Day! W00T! But, even better, April is Autism Awareness MONTH! So all month long we have a bigger chance to spread the word on autism and Asperger's. The President himself actually declared yesterday as WAAD.

So, what are you waiting for, people? Get out there and get it known!

Cigarette Smoke

April 4, 2011 at 5:40 PM

I hate it. Really. I can't breathe around it at all. It makes me gag and dry heave. People get defensive about my sensitivity to it. They tell me that I'm just more sensitive than most people, and so I have to deal. Well, no. It's my health. My air. My breath. And MY nose!!!!!

By the way, standing directly outside the door does not count as smoking outside. Move at least 30 to 50 feet away. What? It's raining? Snowing? Sleeting? Hailing? Not my problem. You're the one who wants to smoke. It's your body, and you have the right. But not with my body.

Oh yeah, and it stinks. I can smell it on your breath, clothes, EVERYTHING. That's not a compliment.

Looking Back:
I still do not like cigarette smoke. However, I have grown to be more tolerant of it. And I'd like to believe that I'm not as rude when talking about it nowadays.

The funny thing is that there was one time I was walking with someone in the park. It was the ONLY time I can remember anyone asking me if I would mind them smoking around me. I was SO taken aback by the question, that I didn't know how to react. I tend to be polite to avoid confrontation, so I ended up blurting out that it was fine.

Erin Clemens

I Love The Library

April 5, 2011 at 1:34 PM

It's so nice and quiet. The books are (usually) in a nice order. Everything has its place, and there is a place for everything. Even for me. And everyone there is always so nice and friendly. What a wonderful place to be! I've been volunteering there for a few years now. It's become a part of my life, and I'm so happy it is. I'm accepted there. I feel the care and enjoy the company of others. I actually read now, whereas before you couldn't PAY me to read a book. It's just too bad my local library isn't funded as well as the better known libraries around.

Sponsor your local library and you can make a big difference in many lives. Because my library has already made a big difference in mine.

Panic Attacks Are Awful

April 6, 2011 at 2:44 PM

And I have been having a few of them lately! Life has been slowly creeping up on me, and I feel like I just turned around to see a mountain of things that I've forgotten about. Things that are usually so easy for me to remember to do. Just simple chores around the house, and in life. The little things have grown. It's so overwhelming. I try to get them done, and I just start to panic. Like, the time is just ticking by, and I didn't even notice.

When I have the panic attack, I feel so hopeless. As though even though I'm trying to work on it all, I just am in too deep already. I have no time for panic. I barely have time to get the things done in the first place. I've slipped up, and I'm having trouble getting my footing back.

By the way, if you've never experienced a panic attack, let me describe it for you.

First way of describing it is by saying this: imagine someone just put a gun to your head. How would you feel? A panic attack is worse than that feeling.

Another way of describing it is literally:

A lot of people think they are having a heart attack when they first experience a panic attack. It feels like you are dying. Once you get to know what is going on, then you start recognizing the symptoms.

Symptoms of a panic attack:

- hyperventilating
- fast heartbeat
- dry mouth
- shaking
- dizziness
- tightness of the throat
- confusion
- tingling sensations
- headache

Note: these are just some of the symptoms I personally have experienced. Everyone is different, and I am not a doctor.

My Teacher Won!!!!!

April 8, 2011 at 2:44 PM

I'm SOOOOO excited. Yesterday, I found out that my teacher won an award due to my nomination! I had to write a small essay, explaining how this person had helped me and others, and why they deserved the award. I'm sooooooo happy for them. They deserve every bit of it!

If it weren't for this person, I may not be here.

Looking Back:
This was a really important event to me. I don't even remember what I wrote, but I do remember that I tried more than once to nominate this person. They were so humbled by it. They deserved every bit of it!

Wacky Windshield Wiper

April 8, 2011 at 8:02 PM

My friend has a windshield wiper that is broken. Well, it still works, but the rubber part of it is coming off. It's weird because when it's raining, and she uses the wiper, you see the piece of rubber flailing about. It looks like a snake. Sometimes, it falls back into place, and works fine. But most of the time, it's just bouncing about. Almost looks like a big black worm. It would distract me, if I had to drive with that. But apparently it doesn't bother my friend so much.

It's certainly entertaining to watch though!

Transportation and Asperger's

April 10, 2011 at 7:11 PM

Planes are loud, trains are loud, and automobiles make me car-sick.

Planes are loud, but luckily I don't usually fly too often. And at least it's not too bad of a noise. My ears hurt, but more due to the air pressure than the noise. Turbulence can be tough, as can the tight space, but again, I can usually get through it as long as I have someone telling me exactly what I need to do when. (Airports are overwhelming.)

I had to take the train today. I really like it, because it is a different experience, even though now I know what to expect, since I've taken it many times. (Knowing what to expect is good for me. It helps me to deal better with the UN-expected.) And actually, it seems the trains have been tweaked up a bit, and so they aren't as noisy. But the occasional squeaky brakes, and the sound of the air hydraulics in the brakes KILLS my ears. So does any feedback on the microphone for the intercom on the train (or anywhere). The other difficulty is not knowing how the train is going to move exactly on the tracks. Once in a while, there's what I'd like to call "turbulence" for the train. When it may shift over to a new track or the track may not be perfectly straight through a section. And you feel like you are on a roller coaster. It would be fine, except that there aren't many handles to hold onto, to keep from flying into someone else, or falling on someone's lap. You can't see the tracks ahead of you (like you can in a car).

Oh the car. The everyday object that most of us cannot make a living without, yet barely have enough of a living to afford. I hate the smell of cars! They all have a distinct smell, and especially when it's warm, it's nauseating. I'd roll down the windows (I love how we still say "roll" when it's mostly a push button now) but then I have to deal with cigarette smoke from the people who think it's ok to let the cigarette hang out of the car window. (It's not!) Not to mention, when you are in the passenger seat of a car, you have no control. Now THAT is enough to make my stomach turn! (Don't tell me I didn't warn you- I'm the WORST "passenger-seat" driver in the world!)

Communication Issues

April 11, 2011 at 7:54 PM

I wish for people not to be upset with me if I misunderstand, and for them to realize how easily I get upset if people misunderstand me. Oh heck, I can't even figure out what I'm trying to say here. Basically, it's confusing and so frustrating at times. And even scary, because I'm afraid of making the wrong move. I hope that they can realize that I don't always just understand what people are feeling. More importantly, I wish that they would not ASSUME that I understand what they say, and then have them be mad later if they find out that I didn't understand.

In order to prevent the mis-communication, I may ask repeatedly if I have understood them correctly. Unfortunately, sometimes I have to catch myself after-the-fact, and hope it's not too late. To explain things for myself, when I'm having a difficult time, I may use metaphors, and compare experiences I've had that may be common to most with what I'm experiencing at the moment. (Such as your first day of school compared to your first day at summer camp.)

Goal Setting

April 13, 2011 at 11:53 AM

For me, personally, anxiety tends to be the main issue for me with goal setting. I have to purposely underestimate my capabilities, and then be pleasantly surprised with how easily I achieve things. When I make a list of things I have to get done, I purposely add at least 5 things I have already accomplished throughout the list, that I can check off whenever I begin to feel overwhelmed. Or, I will break up certain tasks into even smaller ones, so that I can check off more at one time. Such as, instead of DO WASH, I put down: put clothes in washer, move clothes into dryer, fold clothes, put clothes away. Because for me, each one of those IS a task, and each one is a little stressful. This way, even if I only START trying to get something done, even THAT will count. It's the effort that needs to be recognized in myself, not the finished tasks. Plus, if there are a few tasks in the end that I haven't been able to accomplish, then the list of 15 things that I have to do makes those few tasks seem a little less of a big deal. Sure, I can put off a few tasks for tomorrow, if I have accomplished the other 10! For me, I can't just take baby-steps to get things done. I have to go one more level, and take HALF-baby-steps. Not just one thing at a time, but half a thing at a time!

Looking Back:
Sometimes I still do this, but I can usually handle slightly bigger tasks now. Or I may put down the smaller tasks but find myself flying through them with ease. When I get REALLY stressed out, I will go back to using this coping skill. I ALWAYS put a few extra tasks on my to-do list, however, that I have already accomplished!

Wednesday = Art

April 13, 2011 at 10:38 PM

(Author's note: The art class that I attended allowed students to sell their artwork. I offered up some of my bracelets as art to be sold.)

I went to art today! (That's the good news.) The bad news is: not a single one of my Autism Awareness Duct Tape Bracelets sold. The OTHER good news, though, is that I DID sell another bracelet outside of the mall. I plan to continue making bracelets, and I'll see where I am at the end of the month.

Oh, and I didn't have enough time to finish my artwork, but I can't wait to post the picture of the finished product on here! It already looks pretty cool. Hopefully, I'll be able to finish it next week.

Time For A Rant

April 14, 2011 at 9:02 PM

UGH! Long, rough day. Couldn't wake up in the morning, but had to because the dog was barking. Then, one thing after another had to be done. I made a bunch more bracelets to sell, but none sold. Got stuck in a traffic jam on the way to a doctor's appointment, which made me miss my juggling class afterwards. My stomach hurt all day, music was too loud, and there is probably a bees' nest by my animal's grave. And there isn't much to look forward to tomorrow. Or at least, I'm not in the mood to try and think about it, since everything went wrong today. Ok, maybe the good thing is that tomorrow IS a new day. It just may not be better.

Then again, today I DID have a new member join, and at least I didn't miss my doctor's appointment also.

Let's see if I can get more members for this site and more followers on twitter!

Looking Back:
These days may seem like no big deal, but it's really draining for me. It's like having a bad day at work, and then coming home to more bad news. It's exhausting, and many times this is what will cause me to have a meltdown.

How I Keep Myself Calm

April 15, 2011 at 12:46 PM

It's really hard to stay calm when I'm overwhelmed or anxious or just plain mad. But this is a GREAT tip I learned once from a teacher that honestly has worked for me. (Not too much other stuff was working when I learned it, so it was a breakthrough, and always will be my first choice.)

To keep myself from having a panic attack, once I've figured out that I'm starting into one, I have to focus entirely on ing. Ready for the secret?

Breathe in, for 2 seconds, slowly (as slowly as you can, that is) through your nose.

Breathe out, for 4 seconds, slowly (again, as slowly as you can) through your mouth.

It hurts, it's torture, and it seems too simple to work. But it does. It only takes a minute or so to have an effect, if you catch yourself in time. Otherwise, it may take a little longer. But eventually, it DOES work. And it's the only thing I have found that works fast. This may feel like torture at first, but trust me, it is nothing compared to the pain of a full blown panic attack.

Looking Back:
I still use this technique today. I learned it from a teacher. I haven't had a full blown panic attack since I learned how to do this breathing exercise. After re-visiting that teacher, they told me that the most important part of this technique is the idea of keeping it at a slow pace.

Overwhelming World of Smells

April 15, 2011 at 10:10 PM

People call me a bloodhound. And maybe it's because I really can smell a Sharpie marker on a piece of paper after days! The truth is that smells can be good. But too much of a good smell hurts. Such as perfumes, or soaps, or air fresheners. Sometimes, the smell is so strong, that I can taste it in my mouth. The chemicals taste gross. Very bitter. Like getting soap in your mouth. The good news is, I can also smell cooking, and really good cooking is to DIE for.

The worst smell for me is cigarette smoke. I know I have touched base on this before, but honestly, I don't think I ever will be able to explain just how STRONG it is for me. I can't breathe, and I dry heave. It hurts and stings my throat and makes my eyes water.

Hairspray is also pretty bad. That could even make me dizzy. In fact, many detergents or fragrances have the ability to make me dizzy. Especially scented laundry detergent. If I use that on my bedding, I can't sleep because my head is so close to my pillow, which is COVERED in the smell. It stings my throat, and I get a headache.

I can smell the dish-washing detergent sometimes. I stay out of the kitchen when it is being run, because some types tend to hurt my stomach.

I deal with a lot every day, and smells are just some of what I deal with in this world. Remember me the next time you put on that strong perfume, or light up a cigarette.

A Message for Autism

April 17, 2011 at 4:03 PM

I did it! I made it onto a website! www.AutismUnited.org has featured an article of mine in their blog. It describes my life and the challenges I face with Asperger's Syndrome. Here's a copy of it!

If there is one thing I'd like you to know about me, it's that I have Asperger's Syndrome. I'm a 21 (soon to be 22) year-old woman, and life can be a struggle sometimes. I wasn't diagnosed until I was in 11th grade. It took this long probably because I was a female, and I got good grades. However, school was very rough, especially since it seemed to me like not much was known about Asperger's Syndrome at the time when I was there. I nearly had to drop out in 10th grade, due to overwhelming stress. But with the help of the tiny support group I had back then (Thank you Mom and Dad!), I was able to transfer to a school better fit for me, and even graduate. Unfortunately, college still isn't much of an option, because there aren't very many ways the school system can help me right now, and also because I've developed Post Traumatic Stress Disorder from my experience with school. But I'm going to try to find a job, and hopefully even move out into my own place! (Eventually) My true passion is with animals, especially dogs. To me, animals are ranked higher than people, because the animals have never let me down.

Asperger's Syndrome makes life interesting, for sure. I am very hypersensitive to the world around me. I can hear every footstep in my house, or that high tone an old computer makes. I can smell cigarette smoke from a mile away (YUCK!), or a Sharpie marker on a piece of paper after it's been sitting out for days. I can feel that one little stray hair tickling my shoulder, or that tag from my shirt. I can see the light reflecting off of ice-skates, and I can barely keep my eyes open sometimes when it's sunny! I've also learned many ways to cope though. I have a sound soother that I listen to, to cancel out other sounds that could hurt my ears (like the vacuum cleaner!). I use my shirt to cover my nose when something smells bad, and put the air in my car on "recycle" so I don't get distracted from cigarette smoke when I drive. I can cut my hair short, and cut off the tags, and try to find more comfortable things to wear. And when things get too overwhelming visually, I put on my sunglasses, and I feel much more comfortable in my own little visual space.

I want people to know that an Autism Spectrum Disorder is just another way of living life. Please try to accept that these sensations are real for me, and that I'm not over-reacting. I always try to be that person that I'd want for myself. If I am ever rude, I apologize. I misunderstand things, but really, don't we all?

The Problems of Stress (Take 2)

April 17, 2011 at 8:54 PM

Take two! I JUST WROTE THIS STUPID thing and then accidentally clicked somewhere and it all disappeared! It was such a good writing too! So basically, I'm going to make this a bit shorter than I did before (I think). Stress can be a big problem. But I'm not just talking about your average problems. For people (at least for me) with Asperger's, stress can really take its toll, and halt me in my tracks. The smallest tasks, such as doing a chore or going to the store or even getting dressed can be the most difficult tasks to accomplish. In my mind, these things are like mountains. In my reality, they may be molehills, but because I've exhausted so much energy just THINKING about getting them done, they turn INTO mountains. So please, if you notice that I'm getting stressed, take a moment to help me realize it. Send me some logical thoughts, and a few sympathetic sentences, a word of encouragement, and I should simmer down.

Thanks. (Dear God please let this be the last time I have to write this whole thing.)

Erin Clemens

Why I Self-Stim

April 18, 2011 at 12:26 PM

Have you ever been on a really long trip? Felt so excited about something that you felt you just couldn't WAIT for it to happen? I guess those are the best ways to explain what it feels like when I need to self-stim. But I feel this need more than just during times like those. I feel it all the time. I need to clap my hands or head-bang (not like the listening-to-music kind of head-banging, but a gentle banging my head on a cushion or pillow). I need to jump up and down. It calms my nervous system. Don't get me wrong, I still need to stretch after a long trip. But the feelings to STIM are still there whether I'm traveling or not. I suppose that self-stimulation is kind of like "scratching" a "neurological itch."

Looking Back:

My stims have changed slightly over the years, from drumming to clapping to flapping and more. I tend to have a few main stims that I will use most of the time, but can choose from the list of many stims I've developed. I still bang my head on my pillow every night, however. It clears my mind, as if hitting a "reset" button. I have also found that I tend to have a meltdown if I do not do this "head-banging" every few hours through-out the day. For this reason, I have learned that I must allow myself time to do this. Sometimes I forget, however, and I start having a meltdown.

How I Get To Sleep

April 19, 2011 at 12:57 PM

I need a few things in order to sleep at night. The most important things are: my pillow, my sound soother, my stuffed animal, and my music to listen to.

My pillow is more firm than most. It is a Tempur-Pedic. I like it because it holds my head in a comfortable position, and makes me feel safer. So does my stuffed animal (of course!) and another thing that I like to sleep with when it's a little more chilly, which is a heavy blanket. I like the feeling of being covered, except for on my head. Again, I feel protected.

My sound soother is MAJORLY important in getting to sleep. It is what keeps my brain from getting distracted from my relaxing state of mind. Because I can hear so many small sounds, the slightest creek will wake me up. The sound soother keeps a steady sound going, until it no longer registers in my brain, and in fact calms me more until I fall asleep. However, if it is not on a timer, then I can eventually wake up from it, especially if it is too loud. I set it on one hour, and normally I'm fine.

I've listened to the same CD to get to sleep for years. It's been so long, that the track actually has browned due to the laser scanning it so many times. (It's clearly visible. In fact, maybe I'll post a picture of it!) I know every track by heart, and I head-bang to them in specific patterns. The funny part is that I can't listen to this music outside of my nighttime routine, or else I start to get sleepy!

My nighttime routine is very important, and it is very hard for me to sleep without it. I brush my teeth, say goodnight to the dog, unplug my items from charging (because the noise hurts my ears, even WITH the sound soother!!!) put my phone and my iPod on my nightstand, get comfy in bed, and turn on the sound soother, turn off the light, and turn on the music.

I love my routine.

Looking Back:
I still follow this routine. The funniest part is that I still use the same CD as well! Not only that, but it's the ONLY CD that will work in my player. You will find a picture of this CD near the beginning of the next chapter, The First Year.

<u>Don't Touch This!</u>
April 19, 2011 at 7:22 PM

I don't like people to touch my hair, or anywhere on my head, really. The same thing goes with talking to me and having your head too close. I can smell your breath. I can't focus on what you're saying, and that makes me overwhelmed. It's so distracting, and uncomfortable. I really don't like for people to scare me, even for fun. I feel as though people are invading my personal space without my permission. My shoulders are ok sometimes, and I don't mind getting hugs. But the moment you are in my face, it's just too much. All of the body's senses are right around the head. So when you put your hand near my head, I hear it coming. That startles me. I see it, and it's scary. I feel the touch, and I don't like to be touched there. I can sometimes even smell the soap you've used, or lotion, or whatever else you may have on your hands.

And people have touched my hair soooo many times that now it REALLY bothers me. I take time to make myself look presentable, because that is what I have been taught to do socially, and when someone messes that up, I'm frustrated. It's hard enough keeping my hair out of my face, out of knots, and looking presentable. I don't want you to touch it.

And please don't pinch my cheeks, either. Whoever came up with that is EVIL! (Just kidding, but please don't pinch my cheeks!)

Answer (Or Hope To answer!)

April 20, 2011 at 11:51 PM

Amanda asks:

Nice blog :-) my son doesnt (sic) have Asperger's but classic autism. He spits and hits a lot (sister). How can stop this or maybe re direct him? Any reason why he does this?

My answer: (And please, if anyone else would like to have an input, feel free to leave a comment!)

There are many reasons why your son may be hitting and spitting, and the biggest trick is to see what happens **right before** he does this. Is his sister over-stimulating him in some way? Is he trying to tell her something? Or maybe this is a self-stimming behavior he has developed.

Whatever it is, try not to punish him for it right away, but I would suggest that you have him sit in a quiet room for a few minutes, and see if this calms him down. It may take some time, and be sure that the room is one he feels comfortable in.

Is his sister older or younger? How old are they both? If possible, try to help his sister also understand what is going on.

I wish I could see what was going on. Sometimes it's a trigger that needs to be experienced by someone with an ASD to understand completely. Hope this answers your question a little bit, at least.

(**Author's note:** The following was a comment left after my response to the question.)

She is 19 months and he is 3 years old. I know that when she cries it really annoys him and so he hits her. That I can understand. But sometimes she just passes by and he reaches out and hits her in the head. Or he will touch her hair and then pull it, or he will hit her whenever she wants to get a toy he has. I'm really good at managing the situation and having him not hit her, but sometimes he does hit her. I don't get mad at him and I do hold him and tell him that he can't do that. Sometimes when it gets to be a bit too much I will give him time out-- the behavior coach told me to do that. But I stopped doing some of the things she said because he is not like the other kids and I don't think time out will make him understand. He doesn't think the same or act the same as the rest of the kids, and I think for him [a time out] *will be a punishment. I really don't know if it is her presence that bothers him specially* [sic] *when she gets too close to him, or if maybe he doesn't like her getting too close to him. He will also hit me when I say "no" or "later" or he will kick me when I'm changing his clothes, especially his diaper.*

EDIT: Thank you for your comment!

I Have Asperger's

Yes, it sounds like she may be walking too close to him for his comfort, especially if he can reach her. He may ALSO just have the regular jealousy of sibling rivalry. (Probably both.) He kicks you when you are changing his diaper because that is a VERY sensitive spot, and I still remember I HATED diapers. They rub up against your legs in the most uncomfortable ways. Try to find a different brand of diapers, ones that form to him, and have soft, cloth-like edges. Also, grabbing him, unfortunately, CAN make things worse, because he probably doesn't like to be touched. Get between him and his sister instead, and get his attention. Tell him that it's not ok to do that. But grabbing him may distract him from you telling him this, because it hurts and it is scary. Instead, bring his sister away from him. (See if he goes after her, because THEN it may be sibling rivalry.)

Hope this all helps!! And thank you so much for the questions!

Looking Back:

I think this was the first time I realized that I could help others by sharing my experiences. I hope that I've become a lot less "bossy" however, and more "suggestive" in the way I help people.

I Have A Radio Interview!

April 21, 2011 at 11:17 AM

W00T! Tomorrow (**Friday**) at **3:30 PM LONDON Time**, on **104.4 FM Radio**, I will be interviewed about my life with Asperger's. You can listen to it online as well at

www.resonancefm.com/listen

For those in the U.S., it will be 7:30 AM PT, 8:30 AM MT, 9:30 AM CT, and 10:30 AM ET. It will be at 2:30 PM GMT. (And I sincerely hope I got all of those conversions right!)

Please listen in, if you can!

What I'd Like To Say

April 22, 2011 at 7:14 PM

I want people to know that I try my hardest everyday just to make it to the "average" level. And if people would be able to help me a little, by accepting me and understanding what makes things easier for me to live with, they will finally be able to see the amazing person I'm trying to be. I've always tried to be that person, and sometimes it seems that the harder I try, the further from that person I become. I don't want to be seen as rude or ignorant or lazy or disrespectful. That's not what I'm trying to be. I want people to be aware that I just see the world differently, and that I don't need a CURE, but ACCEPTANCE.

Staying Safe Online With ASD

April 23, 2011 at 7:49 PM

When it comes to social skills, let's face it: there is usually a deficit in those who have ASD. And when it comes to the internet, social skills are even harder to work with. So here are a few pointers I would give to someone on how to keep their friend or family member safe.

Give CLEAR examples of SPECIFIC words someone may ask online that would be considered a "red flag," so to speak. Words like "You are a winner!" or "Hey, where are you from?" Even the obvious things such as "I just need your credit card number" may not be so obvious to someone with ASD, unless they know to watch for it.

Give them CLEAR RULES of information that you should NOT give out unless someone (tell them who has permission) is there with them and says it's ok. Things like pictures of themselves, credit card, phone, or account numbers, addresses, their full name, etc.

In case a situation DOES arise, give them specific lines or phrases to use so that if it was really an innocent situation, they may be able to remain social online.

Let them know that if they are still unsure about someone, or if someone online keeps asking them for information, that they should tell an adult they know and trust. (Again, tell them SPECIFIC people for examples.)

Above all, don't be afraid to ask once in a while if there is someone they are unsure about. They may be hesitant to tell you, possibly because they are unsure of their own self-confidence in the situation.

How I (Try To) Deal With Stress

April 24, 2011 at 12:23 PM

As I've mentioned before, stress can be a real issue. Many things that most people can just shrug off tend to pile up for me, and so I've had to try and find ways to deal with my stress. The truth is, I'm still working on trying to figure out lots of different ways to cope.

Here are a few things that I do when I find that my stress levels are going up, and I need to relax to get things done. Because if I get too stressed, I won't be able to do anything.

I try to distract myself by doing a therapeutic activity, such as art or puzzles.

I watch TV or go on the internet and play games or read interesting articles like "weirdest inventions." Again, this is more for distraction.

I listen to music that goes along with what I'm feeling. (Iridescent by Linkin' Park is EXCELLENT for this.)

I walk my dog. (It is said exercise helps to reduce stress. I find it to reduce ENERGY so that you have none left to BE stressed...but then I'm just tired and stressed...)

When things get me really upset, I will call a friend. I have good friends that know that if I call them and say I need to talk, they need to take five minutes to listen to a rant. Hey, what are friends for, right? ☺

If I'm still feeling stressed out, or upset, then I will write. I write basically what I would otherwise be ranting to a friend.

EDIT: One more thing. I found this GREAT website, and if I ever need support, the people there are always more than willing to help. http://forums.psychcentral.com.index.php There's even a chat room!

When all else fails, I realize that I just need some time for myself, and I will go into my room for a while, turn on my sound soother, and just try and daydream or self stim. Or I will go on my hammock or trampoline and listen to music.

The important thing is to try and figure out WHAT is stressing me out first, and if I can't even think, that's when I will work through my ideas. Most "stressors" can be taken care of easily. But for those few that are out of my control, I use many of those techniques to try and keep myself calm enough to deal.

Why I Don't Like To Clean My Room

April 25, 2011 at 1:26 PM

You know how everyone always says, "Oh, I'm sorry, my room is a mess!"? Well, I can EASILY top them. See, the thing with me is that I feel uncomfortable in a clean room where EVERYTHING has a place, neatly put away. I start to feel anxious. I don't know what to do with myself. Everyone ELSE loves it, but I don't. I can't find anything, because it's not where I think it is. I don't put anything back in its place, tucked away. I actually DO have places for things, but they are not your average spots. Like, my laptop belongs on the pillow on my floor, right at the foot of my bed. Now, most people might think "but you'll step on it!" But it's quite the contrary. I KNOW that my laptop is right there. It's there or it's on my bed. And as soon as I feel the wires under my feet, or the softness of the pillow, I stop walking. I have paths in my room, but only I know them. And they change when I clean my room every week. Those important papers I need are under the bag, which is on top of that shirt. It may look like a mess to the average person, but to me, it is my comfortable way of organizing. And, when I DO have trouble finding something, I know the 3 or 4 places that I can check where I usually put it. I hardly lose anything. And it's only when I DO lose something that I realize that "Hmph, I guess I need to tidy a little."

Why does it have to be that 'a clean room is a better room'? It's not like I have mice or bugs. I just have a few more papers and clothes lying around. But it's where these things BELONG. They ARE in the right place.

Looking Back:
I still have a messy place, but now I try to stay on top of it. I have limitations to how messy I will allow it to get before I feel I need to clean it. However, I can still find things in the mess better than I can when it's clean! Once, a friend asked me where my Post-It notes were. I told her to look "behind my computer, on top of the bag that's under the painting." There they were!

I've also finally found a way to clean it that works better for me. I take a picture of the room with my tablet, and then go into a "doodle" mode. Then I circle the items I feel I can tackle until the screen is full of these circles. I can use different colors to circle different categories of items, and I can cross them off when I've cleaned them up. Not only does this help me to stay focused by allowing me to remember which items I want to clean up, but it also gives me a sense of accomplishment when I can cross it off.

My Strange Diet

April 25, 2011 at 8:31 PM

With my Asperger's comes my strange diet. The truth is, I will eat a lot of different foods, but not all together. Overtime, I will go from one food to the next. But my food choices go in es. (Much like my interests, but that's another blog post to come!) I like to eat one or two specific things every day for weeks or even months in a row. My current diet consists of: yogurt granola bars, popcorn (usually store brand), store brand "crisp corn and rice checks" with dark chocolate instant breakfast on top, and thin spaghetti with thin mozzarella cheese, or mac & cheese spirals. Needless to say, my trips to the store tend to be pretty quick.

The funny thing is that I notice that my stomach hurts when I deter from this diet. I don't feel sick (other than allergies) and I'm in good shape. Besides, I love little treats like strawberries and blueberries, or a good PLAIN cheeseburger or a nice steak (YUM!).

I feel that my body truly knows what is best for me, and so I listen to it. And if it doesn't want to eat something, then I won't force myself to eat it. Because it will come back to haunt me.

Social Stuff

April 26, 2011 at 12:03 PM

This blog entry comes from a question from my guestbook:

Rick asks:

Erin Clemens

Hey. I was wondering if anyone could give insight to one of the things I find really hard to grasp from Asperger's. Maybe it's just a particular thing that my wife does, and it's circumstantial, maybe a unique trait of hers. But I find that my aspie tends to be drawn to people who are generally bad news. People who take her for granted upset her a lot, but after time away always forgives them or meets new people who could be considered bad news, or have really negative effects on her. Was just wondering if anyone else finds that? If it's even common? If there is any advice that can be given, or whether it is a unique trait of my wife.

I have been quite lucky in the idea that personally, I am able to avoid this situation **MOST** of the time. However, (and I may be wrong here) I believe the reason that your wife gravitates towards those types of people would be because they DO take her for granted. When you have an ASD, it can be extremely hard to tell the INTENTIONS of people. And a lot of people with bad INTENTIONS tend to act as though they are trying to be friendly. Throughout this process, all I would be feeling is pure confusion, but I would not know what the so called "average" person would do, or how they would react, so I would keep going along with the whole situation. In the end, I would find myself tricked, with the suspect long gone. Your wife may forgive them so quickly because she may not have many friends, and so she wants to keep SOMEONE around. I know that personally I tend to forgive others quickly because I just don't have too many grudges. Life is exhausting, especially when I'm upset, so the sooner I can get over something the better. I have no evidence to prove that this trait of ASD friendships is common, but I believe that it is. My advice to this situation would be to help your wife know why you think these people are bad news with examples of what doesn't seem right and why, and give examples of what a true friend would be doing instead.

Does Asperger's Hurt?

April 28, 2011 at 11:15 AM

Does having Asperger's cause me physical pain? What a great question! The truth is that, yes, it can. The pain usually comes from being hypersensitive to everything, as well as the stress and anxiety of having to deal with everyday life. My ears hurt when I hear a high pitched sound, such as my cell phone charging, or a vacuum, or a fire alarm. My stomach REALLY hurts when I smell something bad, and my throat and nose sting too. The bright sun hurts my eyes, and when I'm driving I usually have to use sunglasses. And when life gets too overwhelming (which it does quite often), I may get a panic attack, and many people say that it feels as though you are having a heart attack when that happens. Another close friend of mine described it as the feeling you may have if someone put a gun to your head, only worse.

The other important point that I should mention, is the need to self stim. Self stimming is my way to release tension, and to "scratch" a "neurological itch." And when I am unable to stim, for some reason, this "itch" hurts too. To get an idea of why this would hurt, imagine having an itch that you can't scratch. (A real one.) Sure, you can try and ignore it. But what if it kept getting worse. What if you had a mosquito bite, or chicken pox, or poison ivy? What if it NEVER stopped itching, and you couldn't scratch it? That's what it would feel like if I was unable to self stim.

So yes, it CAN be physically uncomfortable, and occasionally painful, to have Asperger's. Which is why coping skills are so important for us with ASD (an Autism Spectrum Disorder) to develop.

How Important Is Routine?

April 29, 2011 at 1:51 PM

Kyle asks:

How important is routine to you?

Routine is very important. When I know what to expect, I can better prepare myself to deal with things. I know that I volunteer at my local library EVERY Tuesday morning. So I know I'd better be in bed on time the night before, or I won't be able to focus as well at the library the next day. I park in the same spot, so that I don't have to worry about where my car is, or whether I will get a ticket from misreading a parking sign. On Wednesdays, I have my art class. It is very therapeutic, and so I know that I can afford to spend some energy getting things done before I go to that class, because I will be able to relax afterwards. And when things DON'T go according to plan, I know that I will go right back into routine very soon, and it helps me to deal with the anxiety in that situation. Routines are the key to keeping me calm.

Looking Back:

My routine has changed quite a bit. With the changes came a meltdown or two. But the slower the change, the easier it is for me to handle. Also, the longer I go without change, the harder it is to deal with it when it comes.

Sarcasm, Jokes, and ASD

April 29, 2011 at 9:19 PM

I Have Asperger's

This question comes from Jim on Twitter:

How do you handle sarcasm?

It can be REALLY hard for me to understand when someone is being sarcastic. Usually, I just assume that everything they say is true. I figure that THEY will let me know if they are being sarcastic. And if I react oddly, they can usually pick up on the idea that I may not have understood them. I try to tell people that I don't understand sarcasm, and if I think that they MAY have been sarcastic, I ask them if I am right. Once people get to know me, they realize that sarcasm is not my area of expertise, and they try not to use it too much, or they let me know immediately after, if they were.

Jokes fall under this category sometimes, too. My favorite kinds of jokes are with puns, because I can understand that one word has so many meanings. However, I'm not sure if a lot of folks with Asperger's would understand these kinds of jokes, because they CAN have a different view to them. If you're going to tell a joke to someone with ASD, explain why it may be funny, if they don't laugh right away. I know I'd want to understand. Who doesn't like to laugh?

Following Rules

April 30, 2011 at 2:19 PM

When it comes to following rules, I tend to stick as close to them as I can. I tend to follow them literally and very strictly. If instructions on a laundry detergent say to soak for three minutes, I will time it exactly. If there is no food or drink allowed on the train, I will not bring any. I tend to get upset when I see other people not following these rules to a "T," because I feel as though the work that I have done to follow these rules has been unimportant. Why, when I abide by these rules, is it alright for someone else to break them? Another reason that I follow rules so strictly, is because when I was younger, I was treated as a unit whenever I was in a group. Many times, the people in charge would tell us that we needed to work together, or we would all face the consequences. So when ONE person broke the rules, we ALL suffered. This has instilled in me the importance of following rules, and is a big factor in why I get upset when others don't respect them. A problem with some rules is the clarity in which they are stated. If a sign says "Restricted area," well, how is it restricted? I'm TERRRIBLE with parking signs, because there are always so many different situations mentioned on these signs, and it takes me forever to read them, and so I'm just so worried about breaking the parking rules that I just don't park there. In the end, I tend to ask other people who I trust what is ok and what is not ok. My favorite rule? "No Smoking."

Looking Back:

I have a lot of "Black and white" thinking. When it comes to rules, if I don't know the rule very well, I tend to follow it strictly because I'm not sure what to do (or what not to do.) For example, when I volunteered at the library, I never went behind the desk. I never thought I was allowed to! Then, someone asked me to get some books from behind the desk, and I realized that I could be there.

Podcast
April 30, 2011 at 7:05 PM

I was on Resonance 104.4FM in London! Hear me speak about my life with Asperger's here, Episode 2:8

http://podcasts.resonancefm.com/archives/category/shows/technical-difficulties#

Here is also a modified transcript of the show, questions and answers.

Question 1 - Do you ever feel comfortable? (Part 2: If so, how do you get comfortable?)[Because of hypersensitivity]

There are times when I am very comfy. Usually I am in my bed about to fall asleep. (Or just haven woken up, and wanting to go BACK to sleep!) Or when I'm distracted by an interest, yes. The truth is, that I tend to NOTICE the discomfort more. I get comfortable by say, using earplugs or my sound soother for loud noises. I cover my face with my shirt when I smell cigarette smoke. I use sunglasses when there is too much visual activity going on. Some days, I notice that I'm being even more sensitive than usual, and I tend to stay in my room those days. Self stimming can also help.

Question 2 - How do you cope with needing to stim in public?

I just do it. Or I try to come up with ways to stim that seem to be appropriate in public. I have little things that I will fiddle with that I bring with me. When worse comes to worse though, I just self stim. It's embarrassing sometimes, but the relief I get from it tends to override that embarrassment, and so I try not to think about it. Not only that, but I also try to figure that if someone is going to judge me for what they don't understand, they aren't worth my energy.

Question 3 - You like to be around people, does it frustrate you when it just over-stimulates you?

Yes, it can be very frustrating. But I try to spend my time with people who understand me and can help to reduce some of the things that are causing me the sensory overload. Sometimes though, I just have to leave the situation, and THAT is what frustrates me the most, because I know I've missed out on a lot of things because of it.

Question 4 - You don't pick up on social cues. Can you explain how that affects talking to people?

Well, with Asperger's I can pick up on SOME social cues, so that helps. But sometimes it is difficult to know when I have offended someone, or if they have given me a hint as to how they are feeling. I have to constantly ask them questions like: Are you bored? or Are you angry? In the end, I have learned to cover all of my bases by just saying things like, "I'm sorry if I have offended you, please let me know if I ever do." I try to explain to them what my intentions are ahead of time, and hope that my explanation will help them to understand me better. I truly need people to know that they need to tell me if I've upset them in any way, because I won't usually know. Again, this is why I tend to constantly ask them how they are doing. (Of course, this seems to annoy people too, but eventually I find that if they understand me, they get used to it too.)

Question 5 - Are people without Asperger's getting better at not judging you for misunderstandings or stimming?

Yes-I think. If not, then I don't realize it. But it takes time and effort. I have written a few pieces that I can bring up if I feel someone isn't understanding me well, and I like to use metaphors that will compare what I'm going through to something they can understand better. I look for a certain reaction from people and it tends to help me know whether or not they fully understand. But overall, people are beginning to REALIZE that they ARE judging me. Many do still judge me, but if they don't accept me for who I am, it can be too stressful to be with them, and I don't hang around those people as much.

Question 6 - After all the exhaustion, overexposure and misunderstanding, how do you keep your self-esteem intact?

I have great parents that taught me to believe in myself. To love myself. They have taught me that there are different kinds of people in this world, and that it is ok. That I want to be an individual. And I've seen what low self-esteem can do. It's not fun, it's not healthy, and it's not something I like to have. I don't deserve disrespect anymore than anyone else does. And so I don't allow it. And I believe in karma. Oh, and I do let out my frustrations. I rant to my friends all the time! They just keep me sane. LOL

Question 7 - How rigid is your routine?

Well, I have developed a little bit of flexibility over the years, although it was difficult. I guess you could say that my routine helps me to stay on track, and not so anxious. I like to do a few specific activities, and I refuse to give those up. Tuesdays have been Library day for the past 3 or 4 years. That activity in and of itself has routine. Wednesdays I have my art class. Mondays I now volunteer at my local dog daycare. I try to keep a consistent schedule. But, occasionally, I have to cancel one of these activities. And I can do that, but the truth is that it does stress me out. I guess to answer the question, my routine is flexible, but I can only bend so much for so long before I break. So the less change I go through, the easier it is.

Looking Back:

I remember being SO excited about this, as it was my first interview. Someone actually wanted to know about what my life is like. Most of what I said still holds true today.

The First Year

Don't Change The Look!

May 1, 2011 at 5:52 PM

I have the hardest time with companies that want to change their product's "image" to something new. I end up not being able to find it again! I know that the facial scrub I use comes in a dark blue tube. If that company were to EVER change the name, at least I would (hopefully) be able to find it by the look of the container. But the moment they change the color, the layout, ANYTHING, I associate it as something else that I'm not going to be interested in. I'm great at finding someone in a small crowd because I know what I'm looking for. (You wouldn't see me near a big crowd anyway.) When you change your profile picture, be thankful if I treat you the same way again. It's not that I'm judging you on your picture, but that I don't associate the picture with the personality that I first encountered. Another example might be that: I LOVE the movie The Lion King. And I associate the pictures and colors used within that movie with the movie itself. Because I've grown so close to this movie, I see ANYTHING that looks like The Lion King, and I'm drawn to it. It catches my eye as something I know and love. This is why I can't stand when companies change their products. I love your product "as is." Please, don't make it harder for me to find it.

Erin Clemens

The Best Things About Asperger's

May 2, 2011 at 9:14 PM

This question comes from Brian on Twitter.

What's the best thing about life with Asperger's?

I've taken soooo long to answer this question because I really had trouble picking ONE thing! So, I'll give three:

First and foremost, I love my ability to understand animals so well. I don't know if this is all due to my Asperger's, but I find that I understand them better than most people who don't have it. The reason why I love this so much is because animals are my best friends. They have never let me down, and I feel that I can connect with them on such an amazing level, and I love that I can!

The second thing I like, while also being one of the hardest things, is my hypersensitivities. As much as they CAN get in the way, they can also occasionally be a good thing. I can hear a weird noise coming from a machine when some people may not be able to hear it. It may even be a problem that, if gone unnoticed, could lead to bigger problems. I can notice details in things that other people may not see. I hope that someday, I may be able to prevent a fire from getting out of hand by smelling the smoke before it's too late. Sometimes, I kind of feel like Superwoman.

The third thing that I like about having Asperger's is the opportunity to help others understand what life may be like for those like me who can't speak for themselves. To be able to explain why someone is upset when the average person doesn't know is such a wonderful feeling. I love helping other people, and I hope I can continue to help others understand what my life is like, and maybe help THEM to help make someone ELSE'S life just a little easier because of what I've been through.

Looking Back:
Yes, I still appreciate these things. However, I also have come to appreciate the fact that having Asperger's makes me so different and unique from many others. I can see the world in a way that others who aren't on the spectrum can't.

My Interests
May 4, 2011 at 11:15 AM

My interests tend to go in phases. Don't get me wrong, I have a few interests that I have stuck with throughout my life. I have always loved animals, The Lion King, puzzles, coins, and other things. But for my day-to-day interests, things seem to trend for me. When I find a TV show that I like, I will want to watch that show for hours on end. Other phases may last for a few months, such as when I find a new computer game or book that I like. Some phases have been added onto my regular list of interests, like art, cup-stacking, butterflies, and duct tape. I find myself going back to these things when I can't find another interest right away. Right now, my interest is in autism awareness, knitting and other arts, blogging, and TWITTER (you can follow me on twitter as @AspergerSadie).

My interests in songs tend to be the same way. I have a few favorite bands (Greenday, Linkin' Park, Blink -182-, etc.) but I will find a song that I like and just keep listening to it over and over and over again. I may do this for a week, or I may do this for a month. (Depends on how much I love the song.) Occasionally, I will have a few songs at a time that I will do this with, because one will remind me of another, or another song will pop into my head that I have heard before and I will want to hear it again. What I like to do, is take the song or songs that I want to listen to and burn a copy onto a CD. Then, I can just put the CD in my car and I don't have to worry about putting it on "repeat." Of course, at night, I ALWAYS listen to my one CD, with the same 8 songs in the same order one time. (Enya) You can see the burn mark the laser has made from me listening to this CD every night for almost a decade in the photo below.

Looking Back:

Yes, I still love animals, The Lion King, puzzles, and coins. I also still have the CD, and it still works! A few phases that I went through included studying the life of Amelia Earhart, photography, and snowflakes.

At The Fair With Asperger's

May 6, 2011 at 7:14 PM

I went to the fair today. The strange thing is that as much as I like the rides (really, I LOVE the rides. Better than some self stimming!). I can't STAND the NOISE! The loud music, the squeaking brakes and handles, the people screaming, the vendors calling you into their games, the buzzers blaring, the bells ringing, it CAN be very overwhelming! The other trouble is the people who smoke. It's terrible when I'm trying to enjoy a ride, and suddenly I ride past someone who was smoking. I'm stuck on the ride, and can't get away from the smoke. I LOVE the ride, so I can only be upset with the smoker. If you're going to smoke, please do so far away from other people, especially those on rides! I can't move out of the way of your smoke when I'm strapped onto the ride, so do me a favor and move yourself away from me.

Sometimes it can get too crowded. That's when I try to get on a ride, into my own personal seat, (like the Ferris wheel), or I move to a less crowded section. So besides a boatload of people, a few bad smells (I just hold my nose for a moment until it passes), and REALLLLLLY LOUD music and sounds (I hold my ears around this stuff), I sometimes feel like the sensations I get from being on the rides is worth it all. But I could never stay there for more than an hour or two. I only have so much energy to DEAL with all of the sensory overload, and after that I start to suffer and have a bad time. The trick is, go when it's first opening (literally, the moment they open the doors) and stay for just as long as I can before I start to "lose it" (or no longer have the energy to deal with the stress) and not much longer than that. This way, I can get in a lot of rides in a little bit of time with the crowds JUST starting up. By the time the crowds are at full force, I'm halfway finished, and can use the rest of my energy to DEAL with the negative things and continue to have a good time. But once that energy is up, I'm done. And that usually ends a good time that could otherwise be bad.

Happy Mother's Day, Mom!

May 7, 2011 at 5:48 PM

This is a very special blog post for a very special person. She has raised me to be who I am today. She has taught me to believe in myself, and to have faith. She has taught me to never give up, even when it seems that life is not worth it. Because, she has taught me, that life IS worth it. That yes, there will be people who judge me, who want to bring me down, and try to take advantage of me. But she has taught me that I cannot let them do that. That I am worth living on this earth, no matter how different I may be.

So to you, Mom, I thank you for these valuable lessons that you continue to teach and remind me through every day. I love you, Mom. Happy Mother's Day.

Driving With ASD (Part 1)

May 8, 2011 at 11:08 PM

Part 1 of Driving With ASD comes from a question from Twitter from Lisa:

How did you cope with driving lessons & your driving test?

Well, before I was able to drive, I had to get a license. My parents wouldn't allow me to start driving until they felt that I was ready. Once they felt I was ready, (I was about 17 or so), I had a calm parent take me out to a parking lot for the first time, just to learn the basic brake and gas and steering. THEN, I went to a corporate center near my house that had a large loop around, which served as a "practice track" for me. I made at least a hundred loops, practicing turns and stops and different scenarios. I didn't venture out onto real roads until I knew that loop by heart. Then, I would go out and make another loop around the area AROUND the corporate center. This time, I practiced traffic lights, etc. It was a long time before I felt comfortable to even drive at night. I still have trouble with learning to drive to new places, and I can't follow written directions to anywhere, in case I misunderstand them. So, I usually look the directions up online on a map visually, and use Google street view to see "landmarks" that tell me where I'm at and where my turn will be. I still use this "landmark" technique today. I have multiple landmarks per trip, so if one is changed, I can still see another one and know where I'm going. It has taken me YEARS to be able to drive even a few miles of radius from my home. But I am still working on it, and the good news is that I know my hometown by heart! What's funny is that I don't know many of the road names still, but I know how to get to the bank, because it is down the road from the school and right before the gas station. Get it?

For my test, I was lucky enough to get a private instructor who worked well with me, and due to my following his EVERY instruction to a T (which could be due to my Asperger's as well....) I passed on my first try, even though I stopped at a green light! ☺

This isn't even all of what goes into driving for me. So I will add another blog post about it later!

Driving With ASD (Part 2)

May 10, 2011 at 12:12 PM

Part 1 of Driving With ASD consisted of how I LEARNED how to drive, and get my license. Part 2 comes from a question from Twitter by Erik:

How is driving with Asperger's? (Compared to the average person's experience.)

I guess you could say that it's a lot more difficult to focus on different things. Like, most of the time, I can remember to put on my turn signal, and mainly it's because I learned to do that as part of turning. It stuck, and I can't really turn WITHOUT putting on the turn signal. Also, since you are supposed to use a turn signal when changing lanes, I tend to use it EVERYTIME I change lanes, even if the lane hasn't formed yet. (Getting into a turning lane). The windshield wipers can be distracting, although they are better than the rain. (I usually need my wipers on full when it's a light rain, or else I can't get my focus passed those drops of water!) I have been driving long enough that I can listen to the radio or talk to a passenger when I drive, as long as there isn't heavy traffic, or I'm merging onto a highway. (I NEVER talk on my phone while driving....and YOU shouldn't either...) I don't usually drive with the windows down, because there are too many distracting smells and sounds, and the wind can also be distracting. Sometimes, when I feel the need to self stim while driving, I drum my fingers on the steering wheel. I'm also very nit-picky about other drivers, although I never say anything to them directly. I just notice when someone didn't use their turn signal, or if their headlights or brake lights are out, and other things like that. I do like to think that, because of my Asperger's, I may also be more likely to notice a person walking or a car about to cut me off. (I never ASSUME that I'm better, I just feel better thinking it may be true.) This helps to offset the trouble I have focusing in general, and I know that as long as I stick to the rules of the road (I'm a MAJOR rule follower) then I can be a defensive driver, and a safe one too.

Places I Like To Go and Why

May 10, 2011 at 8:12 PM

Place: The Library

Why: It's quiet, orderly, the people are nice, and you can find information on whatever interests you.

Place: Art Class

Why: The people are fun and very nice, I get to express myself and be creative, I get to be messy and not worry about having to clean up so much. A very accepting place.

Place: Juggling

Why: Again, the people are fun and very nice, and very accepting. You have the freedom to come and go as you please. It's a very positive environment for learning, and I get to show others my own talents as well.

Place: Science Museum

Why: It's always an interactive, hands-on learning ence. The people are friendly and fun, and I've been going there since I was little, so it's very familiar. The museum staff works very hard to maintain an open minded way of teaching both facts and virtues. Another very positive environment for learning.

I hope I haven't forgotten anything……

I Don't Understand: Fighting For Peace

May 11, 2011 at 10:35 AM

I don't understand why people fight for peace. It's an oxymoron in itself! The only direction people will go when fighting is towards MORE fighting. People seem to fight until someone wins, which means that someone else loses somehow. And not the innocent "board game" type of losing. This is major, life-altering (and sometimes life itself!) loss. I believe in a calm debate, as long as - in the event that no one agrees with one another - people can agree to disagree. But to raise a hand or weapon against another being is hard for me to understand. Why do people want to hurt each other? What good does that do? And, doing so in "revenge" is only sinking to the offenders' level. The best way to fight back, in my opinion, is by doing the right thing without harming others. Of course, doing the "right thing" tends to mean that you don't intentionally hurt others. And so if THAT'S true, why do we think that the right thing to do is to fight for peace?

On Osama Bin Laden

May 11, 2011 at 8:42 PM

I didn't really want to do this post, because I like to stay out of politics, but I think it may help others to understand me a little. When I first learned that bin Laden was killed, I was more shocked than anything. But when I saw the whole world was CELEBRATING someone's DEATH, I became sad. I couldn't understand how even some of the most gentle people that I knew were OK with the idea that we KILLED someone. We took someone's life. And while he may have been the reason for thousands of other lives, I couldn't get over the feeling that we sunk to his level. That whether one life or thousands of lives, killing is killing. When I asked people why they were celebrating something so inhuman, the reactions I received, (which I understand better now), were as others might expect. Explanations on the THOUSANDS of lives lost. They talked to me like I was someone who hadn't known about all the terrorist attacks. But at the time I felt that the CELEBRATIONS from OUR side were almost like terrorists' celebrations. FINALLY, someone compared Osama bin Laden to Adolf Hitler. (And I can't stand even typing that man's NAME!) Instantly, images of celebrations I had seen in books and movies flashed into my head. All the images of the end of WW2 that I could imagine. Something clicked. And while I still don't agree in KILLING others, I at least UNDERSTAND what others are FEELING now, and why they are so happy that a man is dead. To top it all off, I had a dream the other night. A nightmare, actually. In it, both Osama bin Laden and Adolf Hitler had teamed up together. Thank GOD, I woke up.

Learning Socially

May 12, 2011 at 8:44 PM

Steven says:

Can I ask if you've been to any social skills courses or such, which have helped you a lot?

To be honest, I have been in a few social skills programs. They didn't help me much, because I am so high functioning. I feel the best way that I personally learned social skills was through experience, and my friends and family explaining to me the situations. Usually they would COMPARE the situation to something I could relate to better, and therefore, I understand more. Such as being angry – I don't hold very long grudges. I don't understand how or why others are mad for such a long time. One person described it to me as an iron. With MY iron, it cools off almost instantly. With others, they need a bit longer to cool down. Now I understand, just apologize (unplug) and give them some time to cool down before having a conversation. I'm still working on just HOW MUCH time, of course.

Self-Confidence

May 13, 2011 at 1:21 PM

Simon asks:

What if anything, would you say has helped you most confidence-wise?

My parents helped by teaching me to believe in myself, and by accepting me as me. It also helps seeing the negative effects of low self-confidence, as well as the positive effects of good self-esteem and high self-confidence. I think difficult times may truly build character. I've been through a lot, but I've come out on the other side, too. All of that, and also seeing how well I CAN do things really helps to build self-confidence. I surprise myself sometimes, ya know! I just see how happy others are when they have confidence in themselves, and I think "I want to be like that!" Not like that person, but with that personality. I pick out what I like in others and try to make it my own. As long as I'm comfortable, I'm happy. I love seeing the effects that even I, myself, have on others! This more positive, confident me tends to make others much happier. And that makes me happy, too.

Please Believe Me

May 13, 2011 at 7:51 PM

Please believe me when I tell you something. I've gone through a lot of doubt from other people in my life, especially during the time I was undiagnosed with Asperger's. It makes me feel like I am wrong. That what I am feeling is wrong. That whatever I do or say or hear – whatever it is – I am wrong. It discourages me from feeling self-confident, and from trying new things. It hurt me a lot when I was a little kid, continuously hearing that my experiences were not true to me. That I didn't really smell or hear the things that I did. That I wasn't really struggling in the world. I feel that I've done everything in my power to make sure that I am an honest person, because that feeling of doubt is so degrading. When I DO tell a lie, I usually don't realize that I AM doing so. Like if someone asks me about something, and I give them the wrong answer. I'm not TRYING to lie, I just don't realize that I'm wrong. So please, I beg for you to believe that what I am saying is true in my eyes, and it may be to you as well!

What Does "Friend" Mean To Me?

May 14, 2011 at 2:18 PM

A friend is someone who wants to see me being myself. They are my friend because they like the person I am, without changing a thing. They accept me, flaws and all. They can be someone I've known for a day or someone I've known for years. A friend will drop everything and listen to me if I call them up and tell them that I need them. They will be respectful, and polite, yet honest. They will help me without me asking them to, or ask what they can do for me. They will listen when I need to speak, and give me strength when I am down. But most of all, they will respect themselves, too. They will LET ME KNOW if I have offended them, because they will realize that I may not know I that have. I will also forgive a friend for forgetting this, as long as they admit they have forgotten. I try to do all of the same in return, and I can only HOPE that I'm a good friend.

On Medication
May 14, 2011 at 11:44 PM

Please understand that I am only writing this blog post because of how medications have affected my life. Medications HAVE helped me. They have helped me become more independent so that I can drive, and they have helped me to get to sleep at night. They have prevented me from wanting to die, and they have given me a little bit more of a life than I would have had if I had not taken them. I'm not saying that medication is the only answer to treating ASD, but I AM saying that I appreciate what they have done for me. I do wish that I didn't have to be on so many. But I have been able to focus because of medication. I have stayed alive because of medication. I have finally been able to go to sleep in less than 2 hours because of medication. And I have experienced what it's like to be on the WRONG medications. It's a matter of trial an error. But when I've found one that works, it has improved the quality of my life. So no, I'm not telling everyone to take medication. But I am telling them not to leave it out completely as an option.

Sensitivity To Light
May 15, 2011 at 2:39 PM

This post is for Jack from twitter, who suggested I write about it.

When I was little, and I had to wake up really early to go to school, the main thing I remember is having to leave my dark room and entering into a bright kitchen. It felt like leaving a movie theater, only it hurt for a lot longer. And at school, whenever the teacher turned the lights on after having them off for a while, I would hear the class groan, but I could never open my eyes right away. It's like looking into the sun for a few seconds. It HURTS. I've never really liked the color yellow or orange. I oddly don't mind lime green, however. But hot pink hurts my eyes. When I drive, I almost ALWAYS wear sunglasses, even if it's cloudy. I love the dimmers on the lights in my house. I rarely put them on full light, unless I am WIDE awake. I don't know if this is all due to having Asperger's, but I wanted to include it, just in case.

Chill Time

May 15, 2011 at 5:00 PM

Conner from twitter asks:

Do you daydream? If so, how do you control it when you desperately need to focus?

I daydream all the time. When my medication has worn off - or as I say, "When my meds are out" - it's really hard to control. But talking to myself out loud tends to help. When I am driving, I say to myself "You're DRIVING!" (Sometimes, I have to say my name to get my own attention!) I also block out times in my day to relax, so that I will be able to have the energy to focus when I need to. These are what I call my "chill" times. I just tell people that I need a break, or that I need to go "chill" for a bit. This time usually lasts for about an hour or two. I need at least 20 or 30 minutes of "chill" time, no matter what. It's **REALLY** important that I get this time to relax, especially on busier days. Without it, I most likely would have panic attacks. During this time, I will play on my computer, watch TV, or whatever I feel like doing. It's my time for myself. Usually, it is from 12 or 1pm until 2 or 3pm. But there are days when I can't get this time-frame, and I have to move it around. I ALWAYS try to schedule it in though, and will turn down events if that's what it takes. I can't be at an event for much longer than an hour and a half without a small break. If it's a longer event, say, 3 or 4 hours, I need at least an hour of chill time afterwards, depending on how much energy the event required.

More On Medication

May 16, 2011 at 12:31 PM

Kate asks:

Hiya! I just read your meds blog, [and I'm] curious about the meds you take to help you sleep. Do you find they have a knock out effect the next day?

Thank you for reading my blog! ☺ Depending on how LATE I take my nighttime meds, they CAN make it harder to wake up. However, I also take meds in the morning to help me focus through-out the day, so they ALSO help to wake me up a bit more. It's been a long, complicated process of trial and error, but with the right meds at the right dosage, I've found a lifestyle that works pretty well for me. It has a few problems for me, but I feel that they have been worth the trade off of the benefits of being on the meds. For now at least. The trick is, that my body has changed over time, so I still find myself going through the trial and error process occasionally. Again, I don't want to preach about taking medication, but I don't want people to completely rule out the idea of it, especially if nothing else has worked for them. It CAN improve the quality of life drastically, but you have to be willing to deal with possible side effects, too. As long as the side effects don't impair the quality of the benefits of the medication, then I feel that meds really help me.

Memory

May 17, 2011 at 11:16 AM

These questions come from Elliot and Luke, respectively:

Do you have memory problems too? (Like forgetting something someone said just a second before?)

Oh my gosh, YES! And it's SO annoying! I have trouble following conversations because of it. Sometimes, it can literally take me a year to learn someone's name. What's funny is that I almost NEVER forget an ANIMAL'S name. I love them so much, and I guess I just repeat their names so many times that I have to remember them. I've been known to call people as the animals' parent instead of by their actual name. (Fido's Mom, etc.) Other times, people ask me to do something for them, and I just completely forget about it. It only takes one little thought to distract me. To compensate during the times that I recognize that I'm having more memory trouble than usual, I tend to repeat what they've said a few times. This doesn't always work, and while I have a million other little tricks that I use (such as writing it on my hand, putting it into my phone, etc.), I still slip up.

Do you remember faces pretty well?

Faces: yes, pretty well. I would remember a face with a personality, rather than a face with a name. That's why I can't stand when people change their looks a lot, or their picture on their profile online. But if two people look similar, even just a little, I can get confused. I remember looking through yearbooks from school, and not knowing anyone's name, but knowing that I'd seen and talked to them before. I still see those photos pretty clearly in my mind. It's funny, that the names that went with those photos are blank to me. I can remember who was nice and who wasn't quite so much, and I see their faces, but I have no idea what their names were.

Reading

May 18, 2011 at 7:40 PM

David asks:

Do you read?

It's kind of a funny story (no pun was intended…at first!) When I was younger, I absolutely hated reading. This is because the words on the page were so overwhelming, I just didn't even want to look at them. I didn't mind picture books, but even the pictures are a lot to look at sometimes. I finally started reading when my Mom found The Baby-sitters Little Sister Series. These books had larger words, and pictures that were nice and simple. I read these for years, until I found other series that I liked. But the thing is, I didn't like any books that I HAD to read. Book reports were always a hassle for me. Then, I started volunteering at the library. Soon books started passing through my hands, and occasionally I'd find one that looked interesting. Then I'd start taking out books on the subjects that I was interested at the time. Now, it's a rare sight for me NOT to have books somewhere. But they are the books that I want to read, not that someone else suggests. The other funny thing about my reading, is that with a newspaper or magazine article, I tend to read the last paragraph first, to get a summary of the whole thing. Then I read the middle, juicy stuff. Then I read the beginning, and find out what the whole idea was about. It's like it's always a mystery!

Stimming
May 19, 2011 at 9:49 PM

Brenda asks:

When do you self stim?

I stim more often when I'm stressed, but sometimes being happy is really too much to handle, and so I stim to let out the energy. I also stim a LOT when I'm bored. It really helps me! As long as it's appropriate, and not harmful, then I say let people do it! I started self-stimming when I was 3 months old, by banging my head against my pillow to get to sleep. (Sounds violent, I know, but it's not as bad as it sounds…) I still do it today, and I turned out fine! ☺

My Special Place
May 20, 2011 at 1:29 PM

Drew asks:

I Have Asperger's

Do you have a special place where you feel totally happy and relaxed?

I love to sit on my hammock, and watch my butterfly wind catcher twirl around. Usually, my dog will sit with me on the ground. I love listening to music while I do this. When I listen to music, it really helps me to go into almost "another world," and block out the things that are upsetting me. It also helps me to enjoy the moment that I'm in, which helps me to relax more. I like swinging to the energy in the music, and letting go of the feelings that I wouldn't be able to express appropriately sometimes. Occasionally, I will run into the problem of smelling cigarette smoke, or having a lot of bugs flying around me, or other interruptions. If it weren't for those interruptions, my hammock would definitely be that special place. I also enjoy the library. And I'm happy when I'm in bed!

Apologizing

May 21, 2011 at 11:30 AM

I remember, when I was younger, people kept telling me to stop apologizing so much. Now I realize what was going on. I didn't understand rules, or social situations. I didn't KNOW that I was being offensive in some way until after the fact, and since I was always trying to be a GOOD person, all I knew to do was to apologize. Eventually, I decided to apologize just in case I offended someone. Then I began to have trouble distinguishing between someone who was still upset, and someone who truly was ok. When I began to see that some people were still upset, I apologized more, because I didn't know what else to do to "right" my "wrong." This led to more "sorry"s for the people who were already fine. And THAT is why they kept telling me to stop apologizing. I STILL have a difficult time with this concept, but at least now I know that one or two apologies are enough.

When I Got My Voice

May 21, 2011 at 8:38 PM

Emily asks:

When were you able to start communicating to others what it's like for you?

I don't remember exactly when, but it was somewhere around 11th or 12th grade. (17 or 18 years old). I remember that, before I could explain it all to everyone, I would use metaphors. Lots and lots of metaphors. I would try and pick things out that I had experienced, and say that it was what I was experiencing. I remember telling someone during a heated discussion that I felt like I was on stage on opening night and I didn't even know the script. And that I had to keep restarting a new script over and over again. This explained the idea about how it takes me longer to come up with a response to someone, and that because I get so overwhelmed with the situation, I can't figure out what I should be saying. (Now I know THAT, too! Yay! Away with THAT metaphor!) Obviously, metaphors didn't always work. Then, one day, I was in another argument, and I just left. The other person was really mad that I had left without finishing the conversation, but I knew that I had to leave or else I would have had a panic attack. I was so FRUSTRATED that this person didn't understand me that I ended up writing a little example for them. I wanted them to know everything that I was feeling, not just the anger, but the panic. (The piece that I wrote can be found at the end of this book. It's titled Asperger's Example.) After that person read it, they began to understand me more. I finally felt heard, which gave me more confi-confidence to try and explain other situations. (My Mom and Dad helped a bit too…☺ Now that I have had more life experience, I am able to better relate to others, and help them to understand me even more. But writing it down in the moment really helped me to explain in DETAIL what was going through my head.

Cafeteria Experiences

May 22, 2011 at 7:29 PM

Jane asks:

Can you describe what is happening in your thoughts/emotions when in a social situation, such as a high school at lunchtime?

Simply put: panic. There were so many people, so many noises, so much movement, so many smells, that I would just panic. I would go into survival mode, and find the most isolated spot I could. Then I would put my head down, and try to go to a different place in my mind. But I could still hear the hundreds of kids talking and even screaming. I hated the feeling of people sitting down at my table, because it would make loud noises that transferred back through the table into my ears. Or kids would kick underneath it. I could feel the vibrations from it all. The pure energy in the room was overwhelming. Then you would have those select few who would bring a strange smelling lunch, and it would make me want to gag. It would fill my nose, and whatever I was eating at the time, I wasn't hungry for anymore. When my friends were there, we had "our" table. We would sit at our same spots every time, and we would vent or laugh at our inside jokes. My friends were usually very accepting of me. (I didn't really tolerate those who weren't.) The worst thing that ever happened at lunchtime was a food fight. I was right in the middle of it when it began. In fact, it started with someone throwing a piece of food at me. I ran back to my table in horror of the food flying everywhere. My friends helped me to stand to the side of the whole situation. What was amazing was that this whole time, I was still undiagnosed. The day of the food fight, I had to walk around with the smell of Ketchup right under my nose from the food thrown at me. I felt sick to my stomach. I didn't care that food had been thrown at me as much as the fact that I had no clue what had happened until after the fact. That it took so long to register that a food fight was beginning. Why was there a food fight in the first place? I just don't understand. It's not like I threw anything back…

Looking Back:

I still remember the confusion of the cafeteria and the food fight. As I think about it, I'm SO glad that I didn't get caught smack dab in the middle of the room during the fight. If I had been caught, I probably would have had a meltdown due to the sensory overload. But I got over to the side just in the knick of time.

Social Isolation

May 23, 2011 at 8:57 PM

Jess asks:

Do you feel that others socially isolate you or do you isolate yourself?

I Have Asperger's

Both. And neither. (Yeah, like THAT answers the question! :P) I guess it really depends on the situation. People who accept me for who I am tend not to isolate me so much. It's usually the people who are uncomfortable around me or people who I just don't get along with that tend to leave me out more. School life was rough. VERY isolating, as a lot of people just didn't understand me. Of course, I didn't really understand THEM either! Which leads to the reason for why I may isolate myself more, too. Social situations take a LOT of energy and focus. I like to have my breaks. My "chill time." Depending on how much energy a social situation takes, I may need to take a break and just re-charge my brain. Take a mental nap. So, yes, some people socially isolate me, but many times I need to isolate myself in order to take part in the activities to begin with.

Looking Back:

I like my alone time. However, I probably ask to get together with people more often than the average person does! There are times when I have asked my friends if they want to hang out more than once a day. One way that I've kept myself from BUGGING my friends too much is by setting up a select time each week to hang out. But for the most part, I'd like to hang out nearly every day! Perhaps the reason for this is because instead of hanging out all day long, I can handle only an hour or two at a time. After that, I get mentally exhausted. So I will take a break, and then another couple hours later, I'm ready to hang out again!

Are Patterns Distracting?
May 24, 2011 at 7:04 PM

Alice asks:

Are you easily distracted by pretty patterns such as wallpaper or carpets?

For me, personally, usually only when I'm bored! When I'm really, really bored, I can get lost in the patterns and may trace them with my fingers, pretending to color them in. But I'm usually only distracted if it's a really crazy or bright colored pattern. Patterns in offices or schools aren't as distracting, but they DO give a focal point for me, if the visual field around me is too overwhelming. A big zigzag or checkered pattern is much more distracting, as is bright orange, yellow, or pink. Sometimes even red. Carpets aren't usually too bad, but again, give me something to study when I'm bored or waiting. Compare it to counting ceiling tiles. (SOME ceiling tiles are distracting, but most aren't.)

My Parents
May 26, 2011 at 12:25 PM

Penny asks:

I'm sure I can speak for a lot of parents out there who would love to know: What do you feel that your parents have done right, and what do you wish they would have done differently?

First and foremost: I absolutely LOVE my parents. I have many people who have told me that I'm very lucky to have the wonderful parents that I do, and I wholeheartedly agree with them. My parents NEVER hit me. EVER. Instead, they would send me to my room for 15 minutes, or take away a privilege. This taught me that it wasn't ok to lay a hand on someone else. (Sometimes they would grab me to get my attention, and it sure did!) They taught me that trust is something that has to be earned, and that it can take time to build it back up if you lose it. They taught me to be grateful for what I have. If I ever complained, they would remind me that some people don't have what I already did, and that money wasn't the most important thing in the world. (It never should be, but I'm realizing more and more that it may have to be at least a LITTLE more important....but that's MY problem...) They taught me to respect them through their respect for me. They respected my privacy, and my opinions, while still trying to make sure that I was making the right choices. They helped me when I struggled. If I got a bad grade, they asked me if I tried my best. (I always did. I was a perfectionist!) So long as I did my best, and worked on improving my weaknesses, then whatever grade I got was fine with them. They didn't force me to do anything unnecessary that I didn't want to do, and supported and encouraged me when I found the things I wanted to try. And they did all of this while fighting for a diagnosis and help for me as SOON as they knew that I needed it. The best part is that they continue to do all of this today.

The only thing that I wish that they would have done differently would be not to assume that the reason I did some of the things I did wrong was to get attention or just because I wanted to act up. I really want everyone to realize that not every "troublemaker" is trying to get attention for the wrong reasons. Maybe, just maybe, they really DO want to be a good person, and just don't know HOW to be. And my parents are already learning how to do that. I know it takes time. ☺

Looking Back:

When I was younger, I didn't understand the expression "just do your best." I thought that it meant that I had to work myself until I got something perfect. This is one of the ways I have "black and white" thinking. I was such a perfectionist, that if I couldn't get something exactly right, I might as well not do it at all. There was no "gray area" in my thinking. Today, I realize that this expression is more complicated than what I originally thought. I always put forth a good effort, but it's hard for me to know if I'm doing "my best" or not.

I'd Like To Mope

May 27, 2011 at 2:07 PM

I'm really having a difficult time right now, so this post is dedicated to myself. I want to mope, but I feel that I need to be strong. I'm tired of waiting for my life to happen. I wish I could just DO things, but I don't have the money to. AND life is getting a little overwhelming right now. I feel stuck. I feel lonely, too. I know I'm not the only one who feels this way, but sometimes it seems like I am because no one will step up and say "I am in that same boat, let's get through it together!" I have no one to show me the ropes that way. I have to figure it out on my own, and I end up getting jealous of the people who are in a better position than I am. For crying out loud, my BIRTHDAY is on SUNDAY. I should be celebrating, or at least having some fun. Instead, I'm just worrying about life, and wondering why I can't have the finances or people with whom to DO anything special on my day. This post may seem really selfish, but hey, at least I'm being honest.

Caring For Kittens
May 28, 2011 at 9:57 AM

Wow! They are so cute, but boy are they a lot of work! My neighbors became foster parents to four, 5 week old, kittens. They all have a respiratory infection, too. Did you know that you have to feed kittens FIVE times a DAY? So every three hours, I'm washing, drying, feeding, watering, and rounding up kittens. And twice a day I have to give them each some medicine for the infections. That reminds me: bring paper towels the next time you go to care for them! (Otherwise, I'm going in and out of the room, and every time, one of them tries to escape.) I made them a little nest, and I'm trying to follow every instruction to a T! That way, if anything happens, I know it won't be any fault of mine.

And it's time for another feeding!

Happy Birthday To ME!
May 29, 2011 at 11:34 AM

W00T! I made it through ANOTHER year of life. It had its struggles, its ups and downs, and its awkward moments, but I've come out on the other side! I'm 22! I had jello cake, with half vanilla icing and half whipped cream on top. I had Filet Mignon (according to a home-made birthday card, NOTHING rhymes with "Filet-Mignon"!) I had baked potatoes and corn. And, as she does every year, my dog helped to start out singing me "Happy Birthday." For gifts, I got an ice-skating gift card, some money (much needed right now!), a gift card to my favorite bakery, a future trip to a sports game, an iTunes gift card, a craft store gift card, a book on how to knit projects for pets, an awesome skull and peace sign bracelet, a wonderful painting I have had my eye on, and an autism awareness necklace! (Gees, I hope I haven't left anything out!)

Good-bye 21, hello 22! Onto another year of mystery!

Looking Back:
I feel old...

Trouble Sleeping

June 1, 2011 at 12:15 PM

Kristy asks:

Do you have trouble sleeping?

Yes. I have to have my routine in order to get to sleep. If I am uncomfortable in any way, it is hard to rest. I can't be hungry, and I can't be hot. I need my pillow, my stuffed animal and my music. Those are just the basics. It used to take me quite a while to fall asleep, and so now I take medicine. I started head-banging (hitting my head against my pillow) when I was three months old, and I still need to head bang to fall asleep. I also need my sound soother to block out the noises that I can hear. They cut into my thoughts as I am drifting off, and wake me up again. With the sound soother, I have one, continuous calming sound that lulls me to sleep. I used to get up in the middle of the night, hungry, and have to eat something before I could go back to bed. I also am a night owl, and I can't get to sleep before a certain time. My body just won't do it. I need my bed to be up against the wall in a certain way. When I'm not in my routine, I struggle to get a good night's sleep. Again, my meds have really helped to make it easier, though.

Goodbye Shed

June 2, 2011 at 1:06 AM

I know this is going to sound crazy, but today I mourned the loss of my shed. It has been there all my life. I don't remember a day of it not being there. Until today, when it had to be torn down in order to remove a dangerous tree. I'll admit, the men came unexpectedly, and I woke up to chainsaws outside my window. It's going to sound weird, but I have actually cried over this. Not the chainsaws. But losing a piece of my past. The memories of that shed will be with me forever. Bringing my bike in and out. The rabbits that would live underneath that my dog would have a field day chasing. The lock that NEVER worked. There was even a window in the back. Pointless. But it was cute. It made the shed feel like a small home. Now, where the shed used to be, is an empty space. A hole where something special once stood. Never again will that shed be there. Because of a new law that says it can't go there again. So now, not only is my shed gone, but another piece of land will be too. It's just a matter of where.

A Bunch Of Other Diagnoses

June 2, 2011 at 9:30 AM

Jack asks:

On your site you say you have "a bunch of other messy diagnoses". What are they?

My other diagnoses are Depression, Anxiety/Panic Disorder (I think I was diagnosed with this), Obsessive Compulsive Disorder, and Attention Deficit Hyperactivity Disorder, as well as GERD, which is basically heartburn and acid reflux. However, many doctors have told me that a lot of these stem from having Asperger's. I was originally thought to have high blood pressure, but later found out that it was due to the stress brought on from school. Since I've been out of school, my blood pressure has actually been a little low! The Anxiety and OCD is usually due to the Asperger's, and the ADHD was my original diagnosis before they knew I had Asperger's. I still have the ADHD as a part of it.

Looking Back:
I have also been diagnosed with Post Traumatic Stress Disorder due to my school experiences.

At A Bar With Asperger's

June 3, 2011 at 10:35 AM

This post is dedicated to my friend, who took me out to a bar on my birthday, and helped me to have a great first experience there.

And to Annie, who has been dying to know what happened! 

I went to a bar for the first time in my life. Of course, I didn't have an alcoholic beverage. (My meds can't be mixed with alcohol anyway.) I remember that it was a little loud, but not as crazy as I thought it would be. I thought people would be dancing on tables, or falling over drunk. But this may have been different, because it was a restaurant and a bar in one. I sat close to the bar, just to get the feeling of what it was like there. They had the lighting really dim, and it felt like it was night. I didn't want to watch what they were showing on the TV – bull fighting. My friend helped me to order and make sure that we didn't get anything with alcohol. The table we sat at was wobbly, so my friend stuck a napkin underneath it, and that helped. I thought that it would be different. Worse. I thought I would be smelling alcohol everywhere, or hearing loud laughter. It was really just like a louder restaurant. I do remember that because we sat next to the bar, I heard the glasses clinking every time someone ordered a drink, and that DID hurt my ears a little. But when I went to make change for a tip, I had to ask the bartender. I had NO idea how this worked! So my friend watched, and kept telling me what to do. I asked how to get into the bar, and she told me just to walk up. I was amazed. You just WALK UP? That's it? Push yourself into an empty spot? No questions asked? Alright then. So when I saw a spot, I grabbed it, but I didn't sit down. I didn't want them to think I wanted a drink. The bartender was nice, and got me some change. I had done it. I had gone to the bar. ☺

What Brings Me Joy

June 4, 2011 at 8:17 PM

Dakota asks:

In your life with Asperger's, what brings you joy that others living without it might miss out on?

I have been told that I am an old soul. That I'm very wise for my age. I like to think that it's because I've been through and learned so much in my life already because of the struggles I have faced through Asperger's. I think what brings me the most joy, though, is when I am able to help someone else speak out who may not have been able to themselves. I can help them to explain what they are going through. Someone who doesn't have Asperger's doesn't know what it's REALLY like. I have an idea, and I can late. That's what people need sometimes. I know I did. So being able to help someone else through what I've gone through makes all the struggles worthwhile. It makes me feel like I have a purpose. And my uncanny ability to figure out what is going on inside of a dog's head is also pretty nice. I see people struggling to understand why their animals act a certain way, and it tends to be something I can figure out for them. Whether it's sounds the owners may not notice, or inconsistencies in the training, whatever it may be. I just love helping others, and if my Asperger's has given me a little extra ability to do so, then that is what has given me a lot of joy.

Swinging With Music

June 6, 2011 at 9:07 AM

I don't know what it is about it, but for some reason swinging seems to be something I see in some people with autism. When I was little, my mom used to push me on the little baby swing, and we would do nursery rhymes. Swinging was the one thing I enjoyed doing at recess, and I would stay on for as long as I was allowed. When we got a hammock, I wanted to go on it all the time. My parents nearly threw it out (it's old and worn), but I'm glad I didn't let them. I still use it to this day! I've always loved swinging and listening to music or singing out loud. I've noticed a couple other people with autism who have enjoyed doing the same. I'm not one to generalize, but I AM noticing a pattern....

At The Grocery Store

June 12, 2011 at 11:51 AM

Going to the store is an interesting process, but very simple. I go through phases of foods that I like to eat. And I won't eat hardly anything else during that time. I know EXACTLY where my foods are in the store. I know what they look like, and I know how much they usually cost. The truth is, a trip to the store – depending on how long the lines are at the register – can last about 15 or 20 minutes. I don't use a list, most of the time. Really, the only time I need a list is when I have more than 5 or 6 items that I need to get, or if I have a recipe for something specific. I feel like I don't need a list, because the reason I have gone to the store in the first place is to get the items that I am out of. I know the items that I am out of, most of the time. What bothers me the most is when things in the store are rearranged, or the companies change the design on their products. If the store rearranges things, I can't find them. At all. I get worried that they don't carry them anymore, and that my routine is off. Same thing when companies redesign the packaging. I can't find the items. It takes me a while to get used to these changes, and it makes my trip to the store a lot longer than I plan for. Another thing that bothers me is when the store is completely out of the main things that I need. When the store is out, I feel like I've wasted a trip. I don't like to substitute anything for what I need. I will try something new, occasionally, but only when I have PLENTY of other things that I need already. (I'll try a new brand of granola bar, as long as I have another quick, portable food to use if the new brand isn't good.) I tend to buy items in groups of 2 or 3, depending on how much of it I already have at home. (If it's on sale, and I only have one at home, I will get 2 more, MAYBE 3.) I get a lot of food that tends to last a long time. That way, if I feel like eating something else for a while, it won't go bad before I want to eat it. (Most of the time, at least.)

At The Movies

June 13, 2011 at 12:18 PM

I went to see Super 8 the other day. It was pretty good. But that's not why I'm writing this post. I'm writing it because I am now noticing more and more that I see the world differently. I mean, I've always known that. But it's standing out so much lately. There were parts of the movie where the audience would laugh, and I didn't know what was funny. I was by myself, so I couldn't really ask anyone. Then there were parts were I would laugh, only to realize that I was the only one doing so. I didn't really mind; it just made me curious as to what the difference in humor was. Why did I laugh at some things that others didn't, and most of them would laugh at things I just didn't realize were meant to be funny?

Then there was the sound. Some movies are ok. But other movies seem to have loud scenes that make every little noise 10x louder. The difficult part is that if I haven't seen the movie before, I don't know when I need to cover my ears. With this movie, I ended up having to cover my ears for half of the film. (Ok, so some of it was because it was a little scary, but hey, I didn't close my eyes or anything!) I wish they could turn down the sound, and put on close captioning. I love watching movies with closed captioning, because if I happen to miss something, I can quickly read it and then move on. Otherwise, I may miss something important, and get lost for the rest of the story. That's why I like wide-screen: the black bars on the top and bottom of the screen are just enough room for the closed captioning, without covering the picture.

The good news for those with autism or others with sensory trouble is that some theaters are now having Sensory Friendly Films. (I think AMC Theaters is a big one in this movement.) The films are shown with the lights on, the sound turned down, and the ability to move, walk around, sing, dance, whatever. I think this is a wonderful idea, but I'm not sure how to go about seeing a movie in this way. Do you have to call them up and request it? Do you need a special doctor's note that says you need such a film to be shown?

Animals

June 16, 2011 at 4:59 PM

I can't stress enough how wonderful animals are to me. They don't judge me, they don't assume anything, and they give me unconditional love. They are there for me when I need them, and never expect anything in return (aside from a bit of food and water, and maybe a walk and a belly rub!) They remind me to enjoy the little things in life, like nice weather. And they remind me of important things, like family. Money does not exist in their world. Their work is for the good of their kind. May it be a bigger nest or a more sufficient supply of food, they get what they earn.

I write this post today because I have had a rough few days lately. But the one constant I have noticed is the love I have continued to receive from my furry friends. My dog has reminded me that it's important to stick to my routine, especially during hard times. She has tried to be by my side, and is understanding when I can't be there for her. My neighborhood animals have shown the same to me. They want me to feel loved. They want me to remember that I matter in this world. That I can get through this difficult time, just as I have gotten through others.

The other day, I went to a butterfly house. I waited patiently for nearly 20 minutes, standing still, for a butterfly to land on me. I sent them a message, saying that it would make me feel really wonderful if they could show me that they love me, too. Then, after the 20 minutes, my persistence and patience paid off. A nice little butterfly landed on my hand. And then it wouldn't leave! It just sat there, enjoying my company. After about 10 or 15 more minutes, it was STILL there, and I actually had to leave! I gently led it to a flower, and it climbed onto it. But I will never forget that butterfly, and how it heard my request for a little bit of love, and was happy to give some.

Happy Father's Day!

June 19, 2011 at 8:00 PM

Happy Father's Day, Dad! This blog post goes out to you! You're the best father ANYONE could ask for. You are patient, helpful, and loving. I will never forget the number of loops we drove while practicing driving, or the hours we spent over math. And when I don't understand something, you always find a way to explain it so that it makes sense to me. You are supportive in anything I do, and remind me that - as long as I do my best - it's always good enough. You are honest, yet gentle with your criticism, so that I know: when you say I do something wrong, I need to work on improving it. Thank you for teaching ME all of these values. I hope that I will grow to be a little more like you. (With a mixture of Mom and me, of course!)

I love you, Dad. Happy Father's Day.

Am I Busy Or Not?

June 25, 2011 at 9:50 PM

I haven't posted a new blog entry for a while now. I figured it was time to do so. The trouble is, I hardly know what to write about. I mean, I haven't been too BUSY to write...I've just had some writer's block, I guess. I've been working on an online radio show, (just joined a group), and I've been knitting and crocheting. But otherwise: nothing. Maybe watching movies. An art project here or there. But I feel like I've hit a block in my inspiration. Which may explain the lack of blog posting. I feel like I've been super busy, but really, I don't have too much to do. In fact, most of the time I'm laying around on my bed bored out of my mind. It's sad, really. It's not what I want to be doing. I just don't know what else TO do. I don't have much money to spare, and I've already done all the free or cheap things. And now, this blog post has gone nowhere. But at least I wrote it.

Anybody?

June 26, 2011 at 6:07 PM

Ok, first, I want to say that for some reason my website builder is not allowing me to reply to comments to my blog. But I did want to thank Jack for leaving me such a wonderful nice comment. I had written an AWESOME reply, in fact, TWO awesome replies! Both times they didn't appear when I hit the "post" button. But I wanted to truly thank you, Jack.

The second thing, and one of the main reasons of THIS blog post, is that I need IDEAS. I need some questions to answer, or experiences to describe, or anything to get me blogging again. I've been off track lately. I've been out of good ideas for a while, now. So, if you have an idea, PLEASE PLEASE PLEASE, leave a comment or a post in the forums. I will try and answer questions (to the best of my ability). But I'm interested in knowing what YOU, the READER would like me to blog about. Try and be specific, because it's hard for me to answer things in general terms. Love you all for reading my blog!

Spammers!

June 26, 2011 at 6:13 PM

Wow! I'm oddly honored! I've already had TWO spammers on my website! It's kind of exciting, because it means that people think that my site is worthy of advertisement. On the other hand, it's kind of scary. How much more spam will I get if I continue? Either way, here is a message to all who are thinking of spamming:

Nice try, but any and all spam found (and I WILL find it - I'm good at finding things!) will be deleted immediately, and the account will be terminated. (Wow, I feel so official saying that!) And if you are wondering what I consider to be spam: if it has nothing to do with my post, or is advertising for something (other than the advertisements that the Webs Host is doing which allows me to have a free website). Just TRY and use common sense, if you can. If you still aren't sure, send me a message and ask. Most blog links will be acceptable. Again, use common sense. I also apologize to anyone if I miss anything that shouldn't be on this site. Please let me know, if I have missed it. Let's all work together to keep this site clean and just try and spread some awareness on autism and Asperger's. THANK YOU!

A Note To My Readers

June 30, 2011 at 12:07 PM

I apparently have a virus on my computer, so I will most likely be bringing it in to be removed. I don't know how long I will be without a computer, or if the virus will get to my computer before it can get it removed. Either way, I wanted to let everyone know what was going on. And let's hope my Lappy-Toppy (my nickname for my laptop) makes it through another virus!

Doesn't THAT post sound like some sort of Last Will and Testament?! Yikes!

Erin Clemens

Breaking Things
July 4, 2011 at 10:38 AM

When I was little (and even still today!), I would tend to break things a lot. I've dented walls, cracked doors, dropped dishes, ripped clothes, stepped on a COUNTLESS number of items, and more. Sometimes things break because I underestimate my own strength. Other times I'm a klutz. But a lot of times, I will break things when I'm overwhelmed and frustrated. When I was younger, I didn't understand that when you are upset, you need time to calm down so that you don't do something you will later regret. All I knew then, was that I was mad, and I wanted to get whatever was making me so angry finished with, because it was usually a chore. When I first wake up, I know now I am too tired to know what I'm doing. I need time to wake up. (I don't drink coffee, but I do take medication to help me with ADHD symptoms, and that helps me to wake up.) But if my parents ask me to do something before I'm fully awake, I have to be careful. When I'm over-whelmed, I have trouble processing things. It's like trying to tie your shoes when your hands are numb. You can move, but you have no control over the laces. You can't really feel what you are doing, or how much strength you are using. But you need to tie those shoes! In the end, you do a sloppy job and your left feeling frustrated and angry that you can't do such a simple task. But, if someone had reminded you to just wait until you have feeling in your hands again, the task would have been a lot easier. When I would break things, my parents noticed that I wouldn't stop trying to finish the task. They had to remind me to take a break and come back to it. Sometimes, if I didn't listen, and I broke something, I had to pay for it to be replaced or repaired. This was so frustrating for me, because I just wanted to get things done and over with. When I finally matured a little more, I realized that it wasn't worth having to pay for something if waiting until I was ready would keep me from breaking it. Today, I still get really frustrated, and occasionally break things, but usually I now break things because I can be a klutz. It's really hard to make myself stop and fin-finish the task later. I don't want to have to wait any longer to get it over with, but I know it's better to do so.

If you know someone who is "throwing a tantrum" while trying to do a task, try to help them relax before they continue. I know I never WANTED to break anything, and felt awful when I did. It's very frustrating for everyone all around, but eventually they will begin to learn that unless they calm down, they will keep breaking things.

A New Poem

July 10, 2011 at 7:36 PM

I wrote this poem this morning. It has no title yet.

It's like a raging wild fire
No one knows exactly when or where it started
But it didn't start on its own.
It started with a tiny flick of disrespect
Perhaps unintentional,
or perhaps through an act of ignorance
but either way,
it went unnoticed
ignored, uncared for, and forgotten
until it caught on and spread
freely dancing flames
slowly, at first,

as if unsure of where to go next
then it found its way
racing and roaring in all directions
trying to catch up to the source of its creator
destroying anything that may get in its way
pain and suffering of the innocent left behind
No time! It had to catch up!
trying to teach a lesson
the lesson of respect and love and care
Until it looked back, if only for a moment
to see the very same lesson it had failed to learn itself
to see its own unintentional disrespect
and even after it has been controlled
and innocence once destroyed has been rebuilt
how can such a hypocritical monster
ever forgive itself?

Looking Back:
This poem is now titled Wildfire. It symbolizes how I feel about my anger and my reactions to injustice.

I Got A Job!

August 10, 2011 at 9:25 AM

Awesome! Okay, obviously, my interview went extremely well! It was with an Animal Hospital. What was cool was that it was the same place I had taken my hamster to. So I knew them already! What was even cooler was the fact that my interview was done in the SAME ROOM that my hamster was examined in! And the coolest part? The person who interviewed me knew someone who WORKED with people with Asperger's! I am SET!

The crazy thing is that I applied for a position that would be EVERY afternoon, and some weekends. I thought that it would be a lot for me to take on, and I would be missing a lot of my weekly routine (I'm an evening person), but I NEED the money, so I just tried to convince myself that I could make it work. I got a call a few days later, saying that the position had been filled by someone else, BUT that the people there wanted me to work with them SO MUCH that they actually CREATED another position FOR me! Now I'm only working 3 mornings a week, and some week-ends. This is PERFECT! (I know, I'm not a morning person, but I'll get used to THAT!) I can still volunteer at my library on Tues-day mornings and get together with my friend Tuesday afternoons, go to art class on Wednesday evenings, and maybe even get back to juggling on Thursday evenings! Almost all of my routine is still in place, and yet I will STILL have a job! It's so perfect! They told me that they loved my enthusiasm, and that I would be a great asset to them. Little do they know, they may just be a great asset to MY life!

Why I Don't Like This Time Of Year

August 14, 2011 at 1:20 PM

1. Back to school- even though I'm not going, I still don't like the idea of it. Seeing all the advertisements, all the supplies in the stores. As if going back to school is something people should be HAPPY for. Why would anyone be happy about homework, get-ting up early, waiting for a bus...etc?

2. CHANGE. I've said it once before (or many times before) and I'll say it again: I DO NOT LIKE CHANGE! It's just so hard to deal with. And this time of year is FULL of changes. Changes in weather, changes in time, changes in routines, changes in clothing, everything! Even food can change. Some things go out of season. And TV shows change too. All those summer programs end with edge-of-your-seat finales, making you wait a year to find out what happens next!

So there you have it. The two main reasons why I don't like this time of year.

Looking Back:

I encourage people to go to school. Due to my bad experience I had at school, I have Post Traumatic Stress Disorder. This is why I cannot go to school...yet. I hope that someday I will be able to find an educational program that works with my needs.

New Routine!

September 1, 2011 at 7:15 AM

Ok, so at least I have a job now. But I really wish I didn't have to change around almost my ENITRE schedule to fit it. Rather than doing the Monday, Wednesday, Friday mornings that I thought I would be doing, my work schedule turned out to be Tuesday, Thursday mornings instead. So the first thing that happened, was that I had to change my day I volunteered at the library. I've been volunteering at the library on Tuesday mornings for nearly 4 (FOUR) years now. So I'm a little sad that while I can still volunteer there (the day has now been switched to Wednesdays), I don't get to see all my regular friends when I go. For the silver lining in this cloud, the library doesn't open until later on Wednesdays, so I can sleep in a bit, allowing me to continue to go to art class in the evenings. The other changes in my routine are mostly due to other circumstances, such as friends starting up school, new projects, etc. All in all, it has been a pretty CRAZY and HECTIC month for August. I can only hope that September is a little bit easier on me!

My Hammock!

September 3, 2011 at 7:05 AM

The other day I was enjoying my relaxing time, swinging on my hammock, listening to my music. All of the sudden, I screamed. I opened my eyes, realizing that I had fallen. The first thing that I thought was "Shoot, am I okay?". Turned out that I just got a bad rug burn on my wrist. (My hammock is on my porch, which is carpeted.) Then I thought "Oh no, did my hammock break?" I was praying that it was only the chain that had broken...and it ALMOST was. But no, it was the HOOK that was attached to the roof, holding the chain, that had slipped out of the wood. (Apparently the wood has rotted all the way through over the years...I've had this hammock for as long as I can remember.) The last thing that I noticed was that my music had stopped playing when I had fallen. I was TERRIFIED that the MP3 player had been crushed, but no, it was in one piece. However, when I tried to turn it on, it wouldn't work! So at that point I realized that one of my best ways to relax (swinging on my hammock with music) was gone. I was in tears.

After a while, I focused more on my MP3 player, as I figured that I would have to buy a new one if I couldn't get it to work. I tried everything on my own, before I looked up some ideas online. But the ideas all said to reset the device, and even THAT wasn't working. Finally, I thought maybe I could try and repair it myself. (I was desperate...I don't HAVE the money to get a new one!) I opened it up, expecting to find the inner workings of the player, and instead found a battery. So, I took out the battery, and put it back in. STILL, it wouldn't work. THEN I realized that a long time ago, my brother had given me a battery for the same make and model I had before (which also had broken, and I ended up just buying another one - the one I was now trying to fix!). Finally, I tried replacing this battery as one last attempt to fix it. Lo and behold: It worked! The only problem was that I had lost ALL of my music and recordings that were on it when I had tried resetting it. I was thrilled that I had saved money, but to have lost those things that I couldn't replace was a hard fact to face. The next day, I plugged the device into my computer to load it up with my songs again, and I noticed that the computer said the player was nearly out of storage. I thought that was strange, and I unplugged it. When I went to see which songs I had on it, THEY WERE ALL THERE! All my recordings too! Perhaps my computer had saved this data, and when I plugged it in, the data was reloaded automatically. Whatever the case, I'm thrilled that my MP3 player now works GREAT.

The only trouble left is my hammock. It's no longer up, and there is no real way to install it again. A free-standing hammock stand would not work, because it's too unstable and I would rock myself too much, knocking it over. So at this point, I am still without my hammock. I miss it terribly. If anyone has any ideas as to how I could re-install it, -that would be great.

Looking Back:
I still love that hammock. I believe I still have it, too. However, now I use the swing in the park within my neighborhood. It's the perfect height for me. I also STILL have the same MP3 player, which is apparently indestructible.

Lots More Good News!
October 21, 2011 at 9:35 AM

There's SO MUCH good news going on right now. Stuff like:

I was a "featured market-goer" in my local Growers Market newsletter.

I was just recently offered a promotion in my new job.

I have been doing speaking engagements about my life and how a certain program has been helping me.

And more is in the works!!!!!

Everything is just happening really fast, and while it's overwhelming at times, at least it's all for a good reason.

Piano!
October 27, 2011 at 2:55 PM

I just recently started taking piano lessons! Basically, I have a neighbor who teaches piano, and she asked me to watch her dog for her. She told me to feel free to play piano or something, and I remember telling her "Yeah, I was just thinking about writing a song soon anyways! Thanks!" So of course, she took this to mean that I knew how to play. Little did she know, I was just fooling around with the keys and the sounds until I heard what I wanted. I knew nothing about chords or anything like that. When she realized this, she told me that she would trade me a dog walk for a lesson! So I had my first lesson the other day, and I LOVE IT! I already made up a tiny piece with chords and everything! I still go by the sound, but at least I know what sounds better. I don't have a piano myself, but she told me that I can practice whenever she isn't home, and that way I can keep her dog company while she isn't there. I can't wait until my next lesson!

It's Complicated
November 22, 2011 at 1:30 PM

Yes, I know, I haven't been keeping up on my blog lately. So sorry out there to all of those who have been following it! The truth is, I have been REALLY busy with work, radio shows, and life in general. My website sort of had to take a backseat for a little bit. And now, well, I'm not quite as busy (although with Thanksgiving, work at the kennel has become CRAZY!) but the truth is that life is still getting in the way. Sometimes things happen in life and you want to ask "Why?" Usually, it's those times when you know you are about to learn some reallllly big lesson in life. But you never really know what the lesson is until it's over, or until you are at least half way through it. Even then, you're not sure what the answer is. In other words, what I've been dealing with is a complicated life lesson, and I know I'm still learning. We all are. We never STOP learning. (Which is just another way of saying: It's life!) So, while I have been trying to learn this lesson, my blog posts were sort of halted. Before, I stopped writing because I was busy. Now I have stopped writing because I'm not sure where this lesson in life is taking me. And now that I write this post, I'm learning one more thing: I will learn more if I write than if I don't. So maybe I should start trying to write a little more again.

If this whole post seems confusing, that's because I write what is going on in my head. And right now, the stuff going on in my head is very confusing!!!!!

The First Winter

Great News!
December 5, 2011 at 5:20 PM

Two things have happened so far since the last time I posted.

1. I adopted a U.S. Soldier. I've sent a care package for the holidays and emailed and snail mailed. AND when I told my soldier a little bit about my life, they told ME that I am a strong an. ME! A courageous hero told ME that I am strong. I'm so honored!

I've been having so much fun supporting the troops! I used adpotaussoldier.org to find my soldier. I liked this site best because it assigns multiple people to a single soldier, so that if one person stops writing, or can't afford to send out a care package, the soldiers will have plenty of support from other people. AND there is NO requirement for how much you support, but it is requested that you at least don't give up on them.

2. When I was practicing piano today (I practice at my teacher's house, because I don't have my own piano), my teacher walked into the room and just told me that I was an amazing musician! That I am one of the only people to have been able to get so far on a piece that she assigned me so fast. I'm so proud! And I only started about a month ago!

Home Remodeling
December 15, 2011 at 12:00 AM

Can I please just say: If there are any parents of autistic people out there who are planning on remodeling any part of their house, HELP YOUR KID!

In our house, we are currently remodeling our bathroom. The good thing is that my parents have been planning to do this for quite a while (probably years, but I didn't realize WHEN they were planning to actually do it until about a few months ago). They started to include me in discussing their plans, even though I didn't have a real SAY in what they were going to do. At least I was INFORMED. And yes, I've put up some complaints, and some whining, and an occasional argument here or there. But I've also learned to accept the fact that it needs to happen. (And I REALLY accepted that fact when the door to the shower started squeaking as loud as a jet engine! THEN I got STUCK in the shower when the door broke....that was when I felt I could live with a new bathroom!)

There is a lot that my parents did to prepare me for the actual remodeling process, because there is a lot of stress that comes with it.

Things that I don't like about remodeling:

The Change- There is change in daily routine, there is change in the environment itself, and it's a LOT to get used to. I don't have much to say about this, but don't let that make it sound like it's not that big of a deal. It's just that there is SO MUCH change that to write about it all is insane for me. (And to be honest, I've been trying not to think about it.)

The NOISE- Construction is noisy, people are loud, and there really isn't anywhere you can go to get away from it all. You can't concentrate well or get things done. We also have a dog that we have to keep an eye on all day, so even if we CAN go somewhere, someone either has to be home with the dog, or we put her in the crate and we can't be gone for long.

Thc TIME- It takes a long time to remodel a room, depending on the size. So not only are we dealing with the previous problems mentioned, but we're dealing with them for an extended period. Waking up early and staying up late to get the things done that you couldn't during the day are the problems associated with this.

The lack of privacy - When you have strange people in your house, or when you have to go to someone else's house, or a public place for your needs, you really don't have a lot of time to yourself. You are constantly closing doors at home, and I have found that driving in my car is the most private time I seem to have lately.

But my parents have really tried to help me through this time, and my friends have been really supportive too. Everyone has been pitching in to make this all go a little smoother for me. And keeping myself busy has helped. I think my parents have really given up a lot to let me have the time out of the house, and to make sure that things that were important to me were not too affected by the remodeling process.

Looking Back

One other thing I remember about this was the incredible amount of dust. It was very thick and it hurt my eyes, nose, and throat.

My YouTube (Tryout)
December 20, 2011 at 11:40 AM

I've put some videos of my songs on YouTube, just to try it out. You can see them here: www.youtube.com/user/erinclem They are all "demos" of my songs.

Holidays and Asperger's or Autism
December 22, 2011 at 2:05 PM

Bear with me as I write this blog entry: the people working on my house have the radio blasting. (Hard to focus!)

Anyway, I figured that it's a good time to try and explain what the holidays are usually like for me. When I was a kid, I hated them and I loved them. As an adult, I love them and hate them.

Being a kid on the spectrum meant that holidays were not always as fun as I expected them to be. I could NEVER wait until Christmas to give my gifts to people, and I hated waiting myself for the gifts that I would get. Traditions meant that I had to take time out of my day to endure the social life of the season. Some of these things I enjoyed. Like the Christmas parties, the inside jokes, (most of which I could understand, but some I don't even remember enough to understand them now as an adult). Even watching Santa going by on the fire truck. (Although, the noise of the fire truck is never fun). But things like waiting for my parents to decide on the right tree, waiting for them to tell me when it's time to eat, waiting for ANYTHING- let's just say I had a lot of sleepless nights! I loved when I was able to get a hamster, because that helped the waiting by giving me something to do. (We had a rule where we were not allowed to leave our rooms until 7am, except for the bathroom!) Anything to DO that helped to pass the time that night of Christmas Eve was good.

Santa played a major role in my life, too. The letters to him, leaving out the milk and cookies (and CARROTS for the reindeer!), listening for sleigh bells, and there were the old times of talking to him on the phone. These were BIG highlights for me, and gave me a little something of relief as I waited through the month for Santa to finally come.

Eventually, I started to get tired of the social parts though. Actually, it was only a few years ago that I finally felt like I was ALLOWED to say "I don't want to do this tradition." Things like sitting still through a movie I might not enjoy. I started to find my own little traditions, because traditions ARE important. They keep this time of year predictable and manageable. But at least this way, the traditions were things that I enjoyed, and they weren't things that I dreaded. There are still some things that my family does that I may not like, but I still want to keep the tradition alive for them, so I continue to participate.

I guess the major thing to know is this: if the child seems unhappy with something that should be considered enjoyable, don't force them to participate. And find OTHER traditions that the child likes so that they don't feel left out!

This time of year should be about giving and caring, but it won't seem that way to an autistic person if they don't feel that way themselves.

T'was The Night Before Christmas (Bathroom Style)
December 23, 2011 at 8:05 PM

T'was the night before Christmas,
And all through the loo,
Not a thing uninstalled,
Not too much left to do.

The tiles were placed,
On the floor with great care,
With two sinks installed,
We don't have to share.

The toilet, it works!
Not a sound of a leak,
The lid is so quiet,
You could hear yourself speak.

The granite is placed,
The cabinets don't bang,
The lights all work well,
And a curtain can hang.

The walls have been painted,
No work Christmas day,
Lots of labor put in,
Worth the effort, I'd say!

But the best part of all,
From the ceiling to floors,
Is the fact that this week,
I didn't have to do chores!

Merry Christmas!
December 25, 2011 at 3:10 PM

And Happy Holidays to all of those who don't celebrate Christmas.

I have to work today. I keep getting people who feel sorry for me that I work on Christmas. The truth is, I love to work. I get to be with animals, instead of having to get along with people. I get paid extra for working the holiday, AND I get to celebrate with my family anyway. It's not like there is anything else better to do. (Everything is closed anyway!) What better way to celebrate the season than by giving back to your community, and helping them to have a great holiday as well?

Now, if I worked at some place like retail or something, then I would not be as happy. But in the end, I guess I would still be thankful that I have a job.

Which I am! ☺

Happy New Year!
January 1, 2012 at 11:55 AM

Wow! What a year I have had! I started a website, and it's still going! Plus, I got a job! (That's still going too!)

Thank you to all of my members, and all of my friends who have stuck with me throughout 2011. It's because of you guys that I feel the reason to keep going with my website! You have all given me the opportunity to be heard, and to be a voice for some of those who are unable to speak for themselves. This is the purpose of the website! To help others understand what my life is like, in hopes of being able to better understand others going through similar issues and triumphs that I have.

Again, thank you all for helping me to create such a successful website for 2011, and here's to even more success for 2012!

Happy New Year, everyone!!!!!

Having Autism or Being Autistic

January 1, 2012 at 8:40 PM

I know that there has been a lot of debate out there whether to call people autistic or say that they have autism. People on one side think that "having autism" means that they "have a problem," so they would rather be called autistic. Other people say that "being autistic" is like saying that they "are their illness," and out of respect should be referred to as "having autism." Here is my opinion:

There is nothing wrong with "having" autism or "being" autistic. Being autistic and having autism mean the same thing to me. I am different, or I have a different way of thinking. Having autism is not a bad thing, and to support my claim I can compare it to saying I "have" brown eyes. Yes, I am different from those who may have blue eyes, but that doesn't mean I have a problem. And it's the same way with "being" autistic. I am not "being" a problem, I am just "being" me. Another way to think of it: having a difference verses being different. Two separate phrases, both mean the same thing. Language really isn't an issue unless you make it one. Focus on the good things!

It's Not That I Don't Care!

January 4, 2012 at 11:55 AM

Sometimes, people ask me to do things and I don't do them. Or I have things I need to do for myself and I don't do them. Or people think that I'm mad at them. Or I say I've had enough.

Let me translate these ideas for you.

Not doing things that people ask me to do, or having things I need to do for myself and not doing them: I may just be feeling overwhelmed, and I know that if I try and get these things done, I will need more time later to relax. It's VERY hard to do things when I am feeling overwhelmed. My mind just doesn't function properly, and if I become too overwhelmed, I shut down completely and go into a state of depression.

People think I'm mad at them: Sometimes, I am mad at people. But other times, I'm actually mad at the SITUATION that I am in. I don't know how to deal with the situation at hand properly, and this frustrates me so much that I get upset. I may yell, slam things, break things even. But it's because I am very upset with the situation I am in, and I don't know how to deal with it. Many times, I truly don't mean or want to snap at people or yell or break things. (I will be honest, sometimes, I really don't care and will break something or yell, but I will sincerely regret doing so later!)

Lastly, saying I've had enough of something: This DOESN'T MEAN that I'm giving up. In fact, often I want to continue. But I recognize in myself a point where I need to stop before I get too overwhelmed. I usually just need to take a BREAK, and then I will go back to it later. The trick is that it has taken me quite a while to know myself well enough to know when I should continue, and when I truly should take a break. But really, I'm not being lazy or uncaring. I'm actually trying to be the opposite! (The sooner I take a break, the sooner I will get back to getting a task done!)

How I Learn To Drive To New Places

January 7, 2012 at 10:10 AM

I have a special technique that I use when I need to learn how to drive to a place where I've never been to before. Actually, there's two ways. One way is to have someone else drive me there once or twice, while I just sit and pay attention to where we are going, picking out specific points during the trip to help me to remember where I am. I call these points "Landmarks," because that's sort of what they are. It might be a fence, or a bridge, or a tunnel, or even just a building. Whatever it is, it's usually going to be the first thing that I notice that will stick in my head. Sometimes these landmarks give me a little trouble, because I have to be careful to choose things that won't change very soon. Once my Dad showed me how to drive somewhere, and one of the "landmarks" that registered in my head was a fire. There was a lot of smoke, which is what stood out to me. The problem was that when we took the second trip to be sure I had it down, I couldn't remember where I was when I got to that point. My Dad reminded me that it was where the fire was, and I knew EXACTLY where I was. Needless to say, I had to pick either a new landmark, or remember that place as being significant. I think I chose another landmark instead, just to be safe. I use these landmarks not only to remind myself of where I am, but to feel more confident that I AM on the right road. I know that if I don't see that white picket fence in another minute or two, and I don't see any other landmarks, I'm going the wrong way. It also helps that I have a really good sense of direction, and can backtrack pretty easily if I need to.

Now, on to my second way I use to learn how to drive to new places. GOOGLE MAPS!!!!! (Again, it helps to have a sense of direction!) First, I find the roads that I know very well. Then I find my destination that I have to get to. I go to the furthest point I know that will get me close to it, and then I find the roads with the least amount of turns that will get me to where I'm going. (I may double check with my parents, because if they know the area better - and they usually do - they will tell me the problem areas, such as a difficult turn or a congested area.) Then, and this can sometimes be a little tedious, I use the Google Street View and go along the new path as if I were driving it. This is how I can pick out my landmarks without actually driving.

As you can see, having Asperger's doesn't mean I CAN'T do things, it just means that I do them DIFFERENTLY. ☺

"Work" Party

January 7, 2012 at 6:40 PM

So, today was my very first "work" party. I will be perfectly honest. Everyone was really nice, and the party was wonderful. It just wasn't my kind of "thing." People talked about things that I didn't understand. They all knew each other better than I knew them all. (I've only been working there for a few months.) The food, I'm sure was delicious, but I just wasn't hungry for it. One person was smoking, and even though they were outside, the door was open so I could still smell it. The whole time, I just felt as though I should be playing with the kids. And the only reason I didn't was because

I didn't know any of them, but knew the adults instead. In fact, I think the animals of the house saved me from feeling too awkward. They gave me something to talk about, pay attention to, and just plain have fun. I mean, like I said, the people there were very VERY nice, the host was AMAZING, but I just couldn't RELATE to any of it. I couldn't process the conversations fast enough, and I had a hard time knowing what was the appropriate thing to do and when. Oh well, now I know how work parties will be.

Routines Help, But...

January 8, 2012 at 10:40 AM

I'm beginning to learn something new about myself. Routines are REALLY important for me to get things done. Without a routine, I'm pretty lost in life. However, there is one little problem that seems to come with being so dependent on routine, which is that any task OUTSIDE of my routine tends to be forgotten. Unless I do something daily or at most weekly, I'm very likely to forget about it. Things like doctor's appointments seem like they come out of the blue. Trying to remember to return an item that I borrowed is like trying to remember what I ate for dinner a year ago. Writing it down doesn't always help, because it tends to get lost in a mess somewhere. I used to just write it on my hand, and that worked great. But now that I have work, I have to look a little bit more professional and so I can't do that. I'm trying to make myself use a calendar, but again, that's out of my routine because I don't always have it with me to write down when I need to remember something. (And it's tedious...) Usually, the best way to make myself remember something is to put it in plain sight, and make it obvious, but sometimes even THEN it won't click right away, or I think "I'll do it later" and then forget. It's a struggle right now, but I'm sure I will learn a way eventually.

Asking For Help

January 8, 2012 at 11:10 AM

Lately, I'm finding it harder and harder to ask for help. It's like, I know I want to do things, and I know I need help to do them. But I don't know HOW to ask people for what I need. So many times people say "You can do that on your own." But then I will try it and I won't be able to do it right. I'm feeling less and less confident in myself, and more and more dependent on others. Sometimes it's a matter of feeling too lazy to speak up, but sometimes I forget, or just don't know WHAT to say! How do you ask people to HELP you ASK people for help? And then people say "Well, we try to help but you just don't like what we have to say." Well, if that's true, try saying something else. I'm making the effort to ask for what I need, and it's not working. So now what? I'm frustrated and feeling a little helpless, and usually when this happens people get mad at me for not taking their suggestions. I need OTHER suggestions! HALF-BABY-STEPS.

Products

January 8, 2012 at 6:35 PM

I think this one will be an interesting topic. It's about my Asperger's and liking certain products. I admit, I have these very passionate likings to certain brands. When I find a brand that works, I just stick with it. I have certain shampoos that I like, specific writing utensils, my usual brand of sneakers or shirts, toothpaste and toothbrush, and in the end, it all comes down to shopping at the same stores too. When one store is out of the brand that I like, I either don't buy anything at all, or I look around for that brand elsewhere. (Usually at this point, it's been discontinued. I inherited this "curse" from my Dad. At least, that's what my Mom tells me.) But because I like my things a certain way, and I don't like change, I will find what I like and keep it. What really bothers me is: (A) When they change the product, either by content or by looks; (B) When they stop making the product all together; (C) When the main company providing the product goes out of business all-together. So that's my lesson to all the marketers out there. If you want me, as someone with Asperger's, to buy your product, DON'T DO ANYTHING DIFFERENT!

Time Management

January 11, 2012 at 12:00 AM

I had this BEAUTIFUL blog entry all ready to post, and I forgot to save it. I lost it. So I wrote up another. Time management is difficult! I have constantly been late to school, work, and even bedtime. Basically, I STILL have trouble with time management. But there are a few things that have helped me to be a little bit better at it.

1. I set my alarm to wake me up about 15 minutes to a half an hour earlier than I'm supposed to wake up. I have to be careful with this one, because allotting myself too much extra time will actually make me LATE. (I'll get caught up doing something else because I have the extra time, lose track of the time, and end up late.) But

doing this gives me a small window to wake up if I "accidentally" press the snooze button...a few times. Of course, this doesn't work with my parents as well, because it wakes THEM up every time, and so I wouldn't recommend this one to those who live with people who sleep in. I also use an app called "Sleep Cycle Alarm" on my iPod touch, and this has also helped me to wake up on time. I started doing this more when I nearly lost my job because I was over-sleeping. Also, I have my alarm clock across the room from my bed, so that I have to get up out of bed to turn it off. This prevents me from pressing the snooze button when I'm still in bed, half asleep. It doesn't always work, but it's better.

2. When I was little, my parents would make me go to bed 15 minutes early if I missed my bedtime. If I missed it again, they would subtract another 15 minutes. I had no idea how quickly this time adds up! I clearly remember going to bed one "evening", and the sun was still up. I thought to myself "Well, I'm not going to be doing THIS again!" Sometimes I still did it, though, and those were the times that I struggled the most because I felt a little frustrated that I couldn't remember to get to bed on time. Now I actually have reminders on my phone to tell me how late it is. 10:30PM, 11:00PM, 11:30PM and at the latest 12:00AM. They were originally labeled with notes like "Stop watching TV" or "Get shower soon" and finally "Go to bed." Now they are just used to help me keep track of the time in general when it gets later.

3. This is the last method I use to stay on track of time. My Dad actually taught it to me, although he told me he regrets doing so, but I don't see a problem with it - yet. I have my watch and my alarm clock set 20 minutes fast. I picked 20 minutes because that's how long it took me (without messing around- which I don't when I'm in a hurry!) to get ready for school. The problem my Dad sees with this is that phones and computers use satellite technology to keep track of time, so that may mess me up. I only had this prob-

lem at first with my laptop, but then I just got used to it. As long as my watch and my alarm clock are 20 minutes fast, I am OK. My phone and my computer are regular times, and I just remind myself that fact. This method has REALLY helped me though!

A Secret

January 13, 2012 at 11:25 AM

This is actually a tough blog post too. I'm going to share a big secret here. Something that I'm not proud of, but I hope will give people a better insight into my mind. I only hope that people don't judge me for this one.

I really, really don't like to make others feel guilty. I feel awful because I know how it feels, and I don't want others to feel like that. But sometimes, I will say things to make people feel bad so that they CARE about me. I do this because of all the times that I feel like people don't care, and it's almost like a way to reassure myself that they do. I know in my heart that people care. But I see people showing so much attention elsewhere, and it frustrates me. It's really hard for me to "share" that attention with others, especially when I feel like what I have to share myself is better. It's a very selfish way of thinking, but at the same time, I feel like it's the only way I WILL get attention.

The truth is, I SHOULD be doing things to make myself happy, and not others. I SHOULD be proud of my own accomplishments. And I am. But I see all of my hard work and my passion being ignored for others who don't even seem to TRY, yet do things well anyways.

So before I end this, let me say one last thing: At least I am WILLING TO ADMIT THIS.

Meltdown

January 13, 2012 at 8:00 PM

I had my first meltdown today that I've had in a little while. (They've been happening more frequently, but I think it's just because I don't have as much to do lately.) But with this one, I knew it was coming. I tried to tell someone, but they didn't understand what I was trying to say. One more word and BAM. I was in meltdown. It was like the straw that broke the camel's back. And it took me nearly an HOUR to get through it. What happened was a mixture of built up frustration, anxiety, depression, and misunderstandings over time. The depression fueled the anxiety making it hard for me to have the motivation to get things done. The frustration came in then, because I knew that I had to get the things done but I didn't feel the motivation I needed to MOVE. Then, when I tried to get everything done, I got overwhelmed, and with that comes miscommunication. Things just DIDN'T WORK. I broke down.

Of course, I feel a little better now, because all of that emotion is out of my system. (Well, most of it.) But I just wait for the next meltdown to happen, and hope that next time I will be able to figure out how to prevent it completely. It's all a learning process. And I'm still in the middle of it!

I Have Asperger's

I Learn DIFFERENTLY!

January 16, 2012 at 1:20 PM

I'm very tired of hearing people tell me that it's not the teacher's fault they didn't understand me. And I'm tired of not being able to learn in the school systems. I understand that teachers have a very hard time accommodating to the masses of students, trying to teach everyone the same thing in many different ways. But all I can really remember about school is stress. And really, is that what you want to teach me?

So here's what would work best for me. TEACH me in a way that I learn best! Personally, I learn best through experience. The problem is, a lot of teachers just thought that I didn't understand the material, so they taught it to me again, slower. That's NOT how to teach me! Not SLOWER, but DIFFERENTLY. Find a DIFFERENT way to share that information. It's like reading: I could read a passage over once, not understand it, and read it over again more slowly, but it's still the SAME. I still won't understand it fully. But then let me HEAR someone read it out loud with passion, and I will probably understand it a little bit better. Let me SEE someone act out the passage, and BAM! I get it! The problem is, the school system doesn't have time for any of this. It's so big that it can only teach the way that the majority learn best. This leaves me, someone who isn't the majority but isn't quite in the minority either, behind.

So at this point, instead of continuing to try to teach me in a way that you KNOW I don't learn, either spend the time to teach me in another way, or help me to find someone else who can teach me.

Special People
January 18, 2012 at 6:45 PM

I was watching a movie the other day. It's called "Push." One of the opening lines to this movie caught my attention. It goes like this:

"There are special people in this world. We don't ask to be special. We're just born this way. We pass you on the street almost every day, unnoticed by most."

And BAM! That's exactly how I feel! I am just special. I didn't ask to have Asperger's. I was just born this way. I don't mind it, and in fact, it's kind of cool to be able to be a little different. But it's true, I pass people on the street every day, and many people don't notice me. That is, until they see what makes me special, and then I stick out to them like a sore thumb.

Searching For An Apartment
January 20, 2012 at 8:50 PM

For the past week or two, I've been browsing apartments online. Just to get a taste of what living on my own will be like. Turns out, I'm definitely not making enough to afford a month's rent. But I decided to go out and look anyways. It was so strange. I felt like I was just "pretending" that I would move out, although my goal is to get out of my parents' house!

Anyways, I think living in my own place would be GREAT! And the ONLY things that concern me are:

1. The one bedroom apartment that I looked at has carpeting in every room. I would need to vacuum, and I don't like the sound of the vacuum.

2. Cleaning: I can hardly clean my tiny room right now. How the heck will I keep an ENTIRE apartment somewhat neat?

3. The cost. The big one. Even the smallest and cheapest places where I live are hundreds or even a thousand dollars out of my budget range. I would need to take on either a full time job, or I would need to take on many part time jobs. I'll be overwhelmed, and then I'll just be going home to an apartment that I have to manage.

Do the benefits of living alone away from parents REALLY outweigh the costs? As much as I think they would, I still don't see myself as being able to do it. I'll never really know until I get a chance. Will I even get a chance in the first place?

Siblings and Asperger's or Autism

January 21, 2012 at 6:45 PM

This is an interesting post for me. I actually just thought of it after posing a twitter question of "What do you love most about your child with autism or Asperger's?" I thought: What about those who don't have it? Like my brother.

Yes, I have an older brother. And he is great. He's what I would call both street smart AND book smart. He also doesn't have an Autism Spectrum Disorder. I can only imagine what he must have thought of me when we were growing up, especially with me being undiagnosed for so long. I know we didn't get along much, but when we did I cherished those times! I must have been so annoying for him. So frustrating. Especially since he is so smart, and while I was getting good grades myself, the rest of my life seemed to be in shambles.

One thing I do know: he accepted me. Or at least put up with me and all of my little quirks. But it truly makes me wonder:

1. Do the siblings of kids on the spectrum understand the situation also?

2. What do the siblings of kids on the spectrum think or feel about their Autistic family members?

3. How do these siblings DEAL with what must be the same levels of frustration and stress, and all of the other crazy emotions that come with the situations, that parents must feel? That's a LOT of emotion for a young child to deal with, and I can barely see PARENTS handling it.

Snow

January 22, 2012 at 12:30 AM

I love the way it looks. I USED to love playing in it. (Ok, so every once in a while I still do!) But the truth is, I'm realizing how much I don't like snow. It's cold and wet. It gets everywhere. It disrupts my routine with delays and frustrating snow removal. It makes me anxious now. This is why I LOVE little flurries, but I hate the regular snow. I have panic attacks when I try to clean off my car, because I can never stay dry and it seems like such an endless task to me.

I'm still trying to figure out how to solve this problem.

Bon Voyage!

January 22, 2012 at 7:05 PM

This blog post is dedicated to a VERY good friend of mine. She is moving across the country and today I had to say good-bye to her. But she was an AMAZING art teacher to me, an incredible house manager at our local theater, and most importantly, a wonderful friend.

Not only did she teach me how to be a better artist, but she also taught me how to be a better person in general. She taught me to take risks and stretch out of my comfort zone.

And she did this, without realizing, even through the very last day. I drove to say good-bye to her at a bar that I've never been to before, further than I've ever driven. That was TWO accomplishments in one for me. (At a bar I've never been to before is one, and further than I've ever driven is two!)

So to my friend (you know who you are!) thank you, and best wishes for a life full of happiness. <3

Hard Part of Asperger's

January 23, 2012 at 8:15 PM

I think so far one of the hardest parts of having Asperger's, for me at least, is not JUST the hypersensitivity or the difference in thinking. No, one of the hardest parts is that I KNOW I have trouble with things, but don't know how to ask for help. It's NOT that I don't WANT to ask. I just don't know at what point I should. And then I see people getting upset with me, and I want to stop them from being upset so badly. I know that being responsible for my own life would solve this. But I don't know HOW to be responsible. When is it okay to ask someone to help you with something, and when is it considered being "lazy"? So I work my butt off trying out ways to make things work, but I can't try things out or get things to work in time.

Like in school. I KNEW that I was struggling with a subject, but I couldn't figure out WHY. I couldn't find what I didn't understand. And then, I didn't know WHEN or HOW to ask the teacher for help. I didn't know if my parents needed to write a note to them, or if I needed to get to school to meet with them early, and how would I get there early... it all adds up. To top it off, by the time I figured OUT that I needed MAJOR help, it was WAY too late. It would be a week before the big test, and I knew NONE of the material. What I needed was someone to WATCH me do the work, and then tell me EXACTLY what I was doing wrong. But I didn't know how to ask for that back then.

Now my problems seem to be in communication with other people, but with other parts of life. Budgeting money, staying organized, how to fill up my life with responsible actions without feeling overwhelmed. But I don't know EXACTLY what I need to ask, or what kind of help I need. I just know that I need it. And until I can explain it to others, I fear that I will continue to have trouble, and eventually have to figure it out on my own.

I guess in the end, the one of the hardest parts of having Asperger's for me is figuring out how to help myself.

DSM Debate

January 25, 2012 at 12:20 AM

I have been hearing a LOT about this whole DSM debate, and that there could be a lot of problems caused by it. I really don't know much about it myself, and how it will affect me. But the truth is, it SHOULDN'T MATTER. I have Asperger's. I have always had it. I don't doubt that I always will have it. It is part of who I am. NOTHING can change that. It's like saying to someone who has brown eyes that they now have blue. Well, call them whatever color you want, they haven't CHANGED.

I'm also not trying to be disrespectful to anyone that this whole DSM thing will be HELPFUL for. I'm only saying that I feel a little nervous about losing things I have worked so hard for. Things like respect and understanding for who I am, and have always been.

I'm not going to say much more on this right now, because as I said, I don't know very much yet. I'm going to see what happens and go from there.

Erin Clemens

Trouble Learning Piano?

January 25, 2012 at 2:05 PM

So I was learning how to play piano so well in the beginning. In fact, my music teacher told me that I was good enough to play in a piano festival! I have ALREADY mastered the song I will be playing. (The festival is over a month away!) But something seems to be stopping me lately. I still LOVE playing. I still want to learn more. But I'm beginning to struggle. And it's not just a little. I've gotten to the point where it's so hard, I just can't get it. I think back to school days, and remember this happening all of the time. I remember that I would notice the problem way too late, and would fall behind very quickly. This time, I think I may be able to work it out. That's because my music teacher was away for a few weeks, and I got to realize that I couldn't do the assignment that she had given. I thought I could do it, at first. But I'm realizing that it's just not working. It's too overwhelming, and I can't read the music and play at the same time. It's like trying to read and write at the same time. My brain just doesn't do it. What I do to play piano is I listen to someone else play the song first, and then I use the sheet music to memorize what notes to play. So the assignment she gave me to play all of these very easy songs is actually harder than learning one slightly difficult song. I know this, because I've MASTERED the one slightly difficult song! I'm going to have to find a different way to learn. Because I still enjoy learning from my teacher, and I LOVE playing, but I just learn differently.

I Can Help!

January 25, 2012 at 3:30 PM

It's very hard for me to sit back and watch other people struggle to understand their kids with autism or Asperger's. I know I could help them. I want to tell them things like "Stop talking! They can't process what you are saying!" or "There are too many people here, take them somewhere else!" or even "They didn't want to hurt you, they just don't realize that they DID!"

But all I can do is watch. I cry inside sometimes, because I KNOW what it's like to struggle. I've been through it myself. I see myself hurting other people, and I never mean to. I just don't realize that I've hurt them until after the fact. Or I know how they will interpret something that I do, but it's not the truth. Like covering my ears may seem to people that I am not interested in what they have to say, but really, I just am so overwhelmed or over-stimulated, I can't PROCESS what they have to say.

It's SO hard because I KNOW that it's rude to tell other people what they are doing wrong, because it's "not my business." I'm JUST "high enough" on the spectrum to be able to understand some social things, yet still be able to relate to the autistic world. Which is why I KNOW I can help people if they give me a chance. I'm SO DESPERATE to help them. I know what it feels like to be in their place. And I know how they can get out of it.

But it seems like no one believes me sometimes. They see me being social, or understanding things that the "stereotypical" autistic person wouldn't. But that's just it. Those things are stereotypes! And while SOME people DO fall into those traits, I don't. But I can help give some ideas to people about what may be going on.

It's what I love about my parents. They have always been SO loving and caring, that they would do ANYTHING for me. Even if that means learning about things that they didn't quite think were true. They are OPEN to hearing EVERYTHING, in case one of those things that they hear happens to help. It's one of the reasons I think we've gotten so far.

So please. I may not always have the answers, and no, I'm not a doctor or any kind of professional. But I have first-hand experience. And I want to help people.

If you have a question, you can send me a tweet to @AspergerSadie, or leave me a comment on my blog or guestbook. You can also watch my YouTube videos at my YouTube Channel, http://www.youtube.com/erinclem

Extremely Loud and Incredibly Close

January 26, 2012 at 12:10 AM

Extremely Loud and Incredibly Close is not JUST a movie about 9/11. And it's not JUST a movie about autism. This movie is more about how a boy who is different copes with such a difficult tragedy. I will say, I DID see Asperger traits in this boy. The "meltdowns" that he had reminded me of myself (at drastic times, but remember, this WAS a drastic time.) The sensitivities he had were similar to my own. Also, the abrupt attitude of the boy struck me as an Autistic trait. But I could relate SO well, that I also could feel his sorrow when he realized the pain his actions caused. I felt the tension between him and his mother as though it were my own. Through all of this, I could only see how the world may misunderstand these actions. It hurts me to have knowledge that I can't share with the world, because I don't know how. The REAL intentions and feelings that may be going through this boy could be easily lost to the everyday person. That's one of the reasons this movie was so hard for me to watch. I'm so glad that I saw the entire movie though. It was truly worth it. But don't take my word for it. See it for yourself, and I hope that you can see it through the eyes of someone like me, because that will make it all the more powerful.

Understand

January 26, 2012 at 1:10 PM

I really get frustrated with people who SAY they understand me, but I know in my heart that they don't. It's with those people that I tend to have more meltdowns than with anyone else. I appreciate their intentions of care and help, but the truth is, they are making it worse. Telling me that I'm not trying hard enough, even when I'm visibly about to have a panic attack isn't good for me. No matter how nice someone is, if they don't understand me, it's just not going to work. It breaks my heart to know that these people just want to help me, but they can't seem to figure out how. I never want to hurt anyone. But sometimes, the truth hurts.

DSM Debate Part 2

January 26, 2012 at 4:55 PM

Okay, now that I understand it a LITTLE bit better, I am OUTRAGED. Do the people in charge really think that to help solve an epidemic, you turn your back on it and pretend that it's not there? I have Asperger's. The only way I have gotten to the point in life that I have is with HELP. And when this all begins to take place, I will lose that help. I will deteriorate back into where I was years ago. So much of the progress that I have made will be lost. All of the hard work for what? If it hadn't have been for the help I received, and the diagnosis that QUALIFIED me to RECEIVE that help, I might not even be here. It really bothers me that what happened to me in school - I fell between the cracks- is going to happen again. Thanks for turning a blind eye on me, to those who think that money is more important than life.

My Dog

January 29, 2012 at 7:45 PM

I'm not a religious person, but if I could get some prayers and positive energy for my dog, that would be great. She has a torn ACL (which is a ligament in her knee). She's 12 years old, so she is too old for surgery. At this point, we are carpeting the entire house rug by rug. This is because we CANNOT let her slip. If she slips on hard wood or tile- anything slippery- she could risk hurting BOTH of her back legs. We are expecting at least a year of complete recovery time. (The first 8 weeks are crucial.) She's not allowed to have pain medication because that will give her an opportunity to feel like she can walk on it, which will hurt it. Like I said, I'm not very religious, but this calls for some major prayer!

MORE Change!

February 1, 2012 at 11:45 AM

There is TOO MUCH CHANGE going on in my life right now! (Actually, I'm lucky that there isn't MORE....yet.) These are the changes so far:

A new bathroom

My dog tore her ACL (no more walks, bit of a change in routine)

BECAUSE of my dog's injury, we have COMPLETELY re-arranged the furniture in my house so that she doesn't slip on the hardwood or tiled floors.

ALMOST had a much bigger change in medication, due to insurance changes.

Cut backs on my service hours with people working with me on life skills and community integration.

And the biggest change of all is yet to come: the DSM-5 change may mean that I won't have Asperger's anymore. And that's just not right.

Erin Clemens

Piano: Getting Better?

February 2, 2012 at 11:15 AM

So I explained to my piano teacher how I was having some trouble practicing. I told her that playing a whole lot of little things is actually harder than working on one medium-sized piece. She came up with an interesting solution to my disoriented practice routine. She used a spreadsheet type of paper with each day of the week on it, and listed each individual assignment in a different color. She also wrote down how many times I should practice it each day. I am supposed to check off the boxes on each day of the week if I practiced the assignment. She also told me that if I can get up to 5 days of practice each week, that's enough.

Now I know how much I should be practicing, so I don't HAVE to be PERFECT. If I WANT to practice more, great! She also cut back on the amount of music for me to practice, so it's not too overwhelming.

The ONLY thing that she says I should work on, even though I personally don't think it will be possible, is being about to read the music AND play it at the same time, without MEMORIZING it. I understand her wanting me to work on it though. Especially when she asked me to play a particular line of the music, and I couldn't. I had to play it from beginning to end. She told me that if I want to be in festivals or recitals, I would need to learn how to READ it, because people (including herself) will ask me to play from a particular part in the song. Now I understand the importance. It worries me that I may have a LOT of trouble with this, but we will see how things go.

JUST Right!

February 4, 2012 at 8:05 PM

I notice a problem in my life sometimes. I get WAY too overwhelmed when my schedule is CRAZY and hectic. If I schedule too much, I may shut down. The trouble is, the same thing happens when I have too LITTLE to do. I just get so restless that I start to feel anxious, and then the moment things come up I feel overwhelmed. The trick for me is to make sure that I always have something planned, and have back-up plans in case something falls through. Of course, I never remember to have back-up plans. Or if I do plan them, I get too anxious to do anything.

I noticed this because this weekend was supposed to be pretty hectic for me. I planned on going to both my favorite museum, AND to ANOTHER museum the very next day. Things fell through for both trips, however, and I ended up feeling too tired from boredom to get up out of bed. Then, I felt too anxious to try anything else.

I think my other problem is that I wait too long for the first thing to be able to work out, and I don't have enough time to do the back-up plan. I also tend to do things at the last minute.

I'm not saying that any of this is a good thing, but at least I know what's going on. It's so hard to get myself not to feel overwhelmed or bored, but well, just right.

Why Do I Intrude?
February 6, 2012 at 7:55 PM

Ever wonder why I jump into your private conversation as if I was a part of it the whole time? I know I do this a lot, and I did it MUCH more when I was younger. I didn't understand myself as much back then, nor did I understand the "social rules." Such as, even if you can HEAR someone talking, it doesn't mean you should LISTEN to them. See, many times my hearing is so strong that I get very distracted by others' conversations. Sometimes I don't MEAN to hear them, but I do. Think of it like being at a concert. Even with ear plugs, you can still hear it. (In fact, WITHOUT earplugs.....YIKES!) For me, even if you are all the way in another room, I can still pick up bits and pieces of a conversation, and without thinking, I automatically stop to listen. I truly think I listen in because it's so distracting. Then, I forget that I'm not actually a part of the conversation, and I will interrupt, jumping in with my own thoughts. I have, on occasion, caught myself before doing this. Of course, I'm the only one who knows this, since it's all in my own little world, and the conversation was MEANT to be private in the first place. I'm still working on correcting my intrusive behavior, though.

A REALLY Crazy Day
February 7, 2012 at 6:20 PM

I JUST barely made it through the day (well, actually, it's not even over yet!) First, I got up and had to feed my dog, then take her outside for her potty break. (I have to carry her outside due to her torn ACL.) Next came the library, for which I volunteer. Not too bad. Then I drove back home and let my dog out right away again. After that, I tried to get some knitting accomplished, before I went to go practice piano. (My neighbor lets me practice on their piano, since I only have an electronic keyboard.) When practice was over, I went back home and let out my dog again. Actually, this time I sat outside with her, so she could have some fresh air. (She also can't be off leash outside, for risk of hurting her leg by running.) Since she didn't seem settled enough, I took her for a short car ride. We got back from the ride, and I continued to knit. (I was trying to finish a project for someone.) Then I had to go and walk my neighbor's dog, and after that I finished my knitting project. It was dinner time for my dog by then, and so I had to feed her and let her out once more. The sun was beginning to set, so I had to pick up the dog doo doo (otherwise our yard is a minefield for when we take her out at night.) Unfortunately, I missed some, and got dog poo on my shoes. I STILL have to go to the pharmacy to pick up medicine, and I hope to watch a movie. Oh, and by the way, I have work tomorrow.

I am STILL wondering how I did not have a meltdown from being overwhelmed today, although I was REALLY close to one. Again, the day is not over yet!

But, That's The RULE!

February 8, 2012 at 7:40 PM

I like rules. (Reasonable ones, of course!) They keep an order to chaos, and I try to follow them. Actually, I try to follow them so much, that I probably go overboard. Take the time that my friend had a chorus or choir performance. It was late at night, and her mom took me to go see her perform. But in the middle of it, I realized it was getting too late! I had to be home before my parents went to bed; that was the RULE! Unfortunately, I ended up cutting my friend's performance short because I INSISTED I needed to be home. Of course, I didn't HAVE to. My parents told me I would have been fine because I was with an adult that they knew. But to me, that wasn't consistent with the rule, and I didn't know there could be exceptions.

Another time, and this was more recently, my friend wanted to go ice skating with me. But he's not allowed to drive me, I thought. So I had to tell him no. (I didn't have access to a car at this point.) Later, I was asking my mom if she could drive me there to meet him, and she asked me, "Why can't HE drive you?". WHAT? But that's NOT the RULE! I told her "I thought I couldn't!" She explained that she had put that rule in place YEARS ago, when he had FIRST gotten his driver's license. Apparently, at some point in those years, he had gained enough skill to drive me. But I didn't know that. And I didn't know to ASK when this would happen. All I knew was, well, I couldn't ride with him, and that was the rule.

So you see, I like rules. Concrete rules with HARDLY any exception. (I mean, I don't mind giving people a LITTLE break here or there, but really, follow the rules!) So when OTHER people break them, I get upset. Especially when they GET AWAY with them. I follow the rules. And I usually don't forget them.

The Oreo Cookie Technique
February 16, 2012 at 7:30 PM

I have a little tip for everyone out there. When I want to offer constructive criticism, I use something that I like to call the "Oreo Cookie Technique." This is where you first address something that you like about the subject. Start out positive. Then, you squeeze in the complaint or problem, making it sound as simple and polite as possible. Finally, end with saying another positive thing, or rephrasing the first positive thing that you stated.

An example:

Cookie: I think you are doing a wonderful job with cleaning your room.

Cream: I think it may smell even better if you did your laundry a little more often.

Cookie: But again, your room is looking great!

So there you have it! And it works almost every time, from my experience using it with others.

Awesome Week!
February 18, 2012 at 11:00 AM

I have had SUCH an awesome week! I think it started with getting a good night's sleep, too! (Sleep is VERY important people!) After about 2 weeks of being sleep deprived from having to stay up late to let my dog out (we have to carry her out because she has a torn ACL) and getting up early to let her out again before going to work, I finally got a few nights of decent sleep. I will thank my Dad for this BIG TIME, because he saw how desperate I was getting for rest, and for a few nights he got up to let the dog out, so I could get to bed early. Oh my gosh, it's nice to sleep well!

On Valentine's Day, after failing to receive a Valentine since 5th grade, I got a beautiful Valentine from a good friend. (Hugs to them!)

The next thing that happened was also wonderful: Autism Speaks listed my blog on their website! HUGE thanks to Autism Speaks for sharing my work!

Then, after about a few WEEKS of searching for an awesome new hoodie that I had seen but thought had sold out, I went back to check one more time and (credit to my friend) found it! I'm SO happy because I couldn't find it ANYWHERE online. It's the only really AWESOME looking blue hoodie with built in headphones that I could find in stores. I thought it was gone forever, and I would have to settle for something else, but W00T! I got it! (I like the built in headphones not just to play music with, but it helps to use them as ear plugs if I find myself at a place that is too loud.)

Continuing on in the week, I finally saved up enough money, not just to pay off my enormous car repair bill (that my parents graciously loaned me the money for, with an agreement that I would pay them back by a certain time), but also to finally make a hair appointment to get two streaks of blue in my hair. I have wanted those blue streaks for about a year now!

And to end the week, I have a speaking engagement about my life with Asperger's, and then I get to go to my favorite museum!

Oh yeah, and let's not forget that I got to watch my favorite movie of all time, *The Lion King*, with the best kid to babysit for. Yeah, it's been an AWESOME week.

Personal Space

February 19, 2012 at 7:25 PM

I just recently had someone ask me a question about how to help their child learn about the idea of personal space. This was a tough question for me, at first. I had to really think about how I myself came to understand why people need that little bubble of protection. It actually brought me back to middle school years, when I went on a field trip. There was a demonstration where a man drew 3 circles on the ground, each inside the other, a specific distance apart. Then he asked a student to stand in the center one. He walked into the first, outer circle himself, and we all just stared, bored. Then he walked into the closer, second one. Okay, interesting. Would he really walk into the 3rd one, and get THAT close to this student? He did. And THAT is when I learned how important personal space is. It's not JUST about comfort, but safety, too. And I will never forget how he pointed out that the student felt the need to back away when he walked into the 3rd one. It was pure instinct that the student did this. I really like this way for explaining the need for personal space to me, because it was a very visual and experiential way of learning the importance of a social skill. And it worked. (I also remember I was happy at the time because I was allowed to eat lunch, and I was STARVING!)

If you want to try this experiment with your own child, you can easily find a diagram of the circles on Google by searching "personal space." Just use some sidewalk chalk and try it yourself! ☺

Coming Down On Medication

February 21, 2012 at 6:30 PM

A word on medication: PLEASE be VERY CAREFUL! (Also, I am NOT a doctor, and this is not intended to be used as medical or professional advice.)

I am on the medication called Abilify. My psychiatrist wanted me to go up from 2 milligrams to 3 milligrams to see if my sense of feeling overwhelmed would go down. Well, yes, it did. However, I was feeling way too sleepy during the day, napping whenever I had some free time. I took the 3 milligrams for about a week, and then decided that I didn't like feeling so tired, so I went back down to 2 milligrams. On my own.

Without consulting my doctor first.

The result? About 3 or 4 days later, I have a near panic attack (a moment when I FEEL like I'm going to have a panic attack, but stop it from occurring) in the morning, and then feel overwhelmed and panicky for the rest of the day.

Now I have always known that you don't just STOP taking medication, especially anti-depression medication. However, never in my dreams did I imagine that the small change in my dosage, which was really just going back down to my ORIGINAL dose in the first place, could ALSO cause such a big problem. In fact, I really didn't think it was going to make that big of a difference. I thought I would just simply go back to how I felt before I raised my dosage. (In other words, I would just be more awake again.)

So please, I have learned my lesson. I hope I can help others to learn something important here, too. Consult your doctor, even if you think you know it's fine. Just double check, anyways. No matter what, if you make a change in medication, tell your doctor before you do it. You may be surprised. At least you won't have to find out the hard way, like I have. (And I don't blame my doc for this at all. It was all MY doing.)

Getting My Hair Done

February 23, 2012 at 3:55 PM

(Note, at the end of this post I have listed some tips for others who may be thinking of having their child or family member with ASD get their hair done.)

Well, today was certainly an experience! I got my hair dyed with two streaks of blue. (Yes, I love the color blue.) I had been planning to do this for at least a year now, so the whole aspect of "change" didn't bother me. In fact, I've even been using blue hair extensions for most of that time.

No, the change didn't bother me. But I was still REALLY worried that I wouldn't like the experience. I mean, I don't like people touching my head, which is why I only get my hair cut once a year in the first place. I do like my hairdresser though. She's reallllly nice! I was really worried though, about a few things. First, the smell. Yes, it smelled bad, but it wasn't QUITE as bad as I thought it would be. And actually, it smelled GOOD towards the end, because the hair dye that was used was scented BLUEBERRY! So thankfully, the smell wasn't too bad. The second thing I was worried about was whether or not I would still be able to use my special conditioner. (I LOVE my conditioner. It makes my hair feel good and has a nice calming scent to it.) As it turns out, using conditioner is GOOD for my dyed hair. PERFECT! On to problem number three. I don't like heat. I really don't like the hair dryer. This was the only thing that didn't work out sooo well for me because apparently heat is what makes the dye adhere. I was able to get through that part only by reminding myself that I wanted blue hair. (And my hairdresser asked me if it was burning me, and I said yes.)

So if you want a few tips for helping someone with autism or Asperger's to get their hair done, here you go:

1. Keep asking me if the hairdryer is too hot, cold, in my eyes, itchy, etc. Sometimes, I won't speak up on my own. And even if I say no the first time, keep asking. I may say yes at some point!

2. Explain EVERYTHING. I can't SEE what they are doing all of the time, especially to the back of my head. Let me know that they are putting in a clip, or if they are going to cut close to my ear or neck. Those are really sensitive spots that need to be respected!

3. Please be gentle. No roughing up my hair, pulling hard, etc. If they can move quickly and still be gentle, that's even better.

4. Talking. I personally like it, because it's something to do when I'm feeling a bit uncomfortable, and I'm a talkative person anyways. But for others it may be too much stimulation. It may overwhelm. So start out slow, and if it seems to help, great. Otherwise, keep the talking to a minimum.

Financial Frustration!
February 26, 2012 at 9:50 PM

My Dad told me I should be really proud of my accomplishment of paying off my HUGE car repair bill. I WOULD be proud, if I could find a way to STICK TO this routine that I used to get to the payoff. The routine was that I would pay $50 a month to my Dad and in turn he would pay for my car repair. Then I would save the money that I need for gas each month, and for my phone, and have the rest leftover for fun spending. I figured that once I paid off the repair, I could just keep setting aside money, even if it was only $30 instead of $50. This way, I could actually save up money, and reward myself for paying off the bill with some extra spending money.

The problem with this idea: LIFE! First off, RIGHT before I paid off my car repair bill, the check engine light came on. I still don't know why, and the light hasn't come back on, but I dread turning my car on every time now. Second, I need an oil change, which means that the very first month after I have paid off the bill, I will STILL have to spend almost $50 anyway. So even though I accomplished the huge bill payment, I have nothing to reward myself with financially. Third, and most annoying, the gas prices have JUMPED since I started this routine budget. Instead of having my usual extra cash at the end of paying my bills, it mostly goes towards gas.

So, to be honest, I'm feeling very frustrated and depressed with trying to find a way to manage my money. I just can't seem to get a financial foot on the ground, no matter how hard I try. I should be happy that I have a car, that I'm not in debt, etc. But instead I feel like I'm fighting to stay afloat. It makes me just want to say "forget it!" I almost need a head start or something. Just a big chunk that I can put away and save so I at least have that little cushion. But I can't even build that up.

I hate writing depressing blog posts, but at least I'm being honest.

Change: Easy or Hard?

February 28, 2012 at 8:10 PM

I know, I've posted many times about how hard change is for me to deal with. I swear that I'm not lying when I say that it's hard! Usually, things for me need to change VERY gradually, and I must have many options to choose from for it to work. However, there ARE times when change IS good. I surprise myself, too.

For instance, my room. For the first, say, 13 or 14 years of my life, I liked only the color purple, and had all of my furniture laid out the same way. Then, out of the blue, I felt the need to change it. My favorite colors changed to blue (any shade), lime green, and purple. (Purple has since left my "favorite colors" category.) Then, ALL of my furniture moved around. The funny thing is, I'm 22 years old now, and I haven't changed it again since.

Here's another care where I find change easy to accept: When the change MUST happen in order for me to get what I want. Like with my dog. She tore her ACL, and we had to re-arrange the ENTIRE living and dining room. If I didn't care so much about my dog, the change most definitely would have been harder to deal with.

Another example for change having to happen to get what I want is with my hair. I wanted my hair dyed with streaks of blue, because

I LOVED how it looked when I used extensions. (The extensions started pulling my hair out, so I couldn't use them anymore.) I have dyed it, but with this came some change in routine. My shower is no longer: wash hair, use soap, use conditioner, use facial scrub. Now it's: use soap, use facial scrub, and EVERY OTHER DAY use SPECIAL shampoo and conditioner under cold water with faucet, dry hair, then get back in and use soap and facial scrub. It's a major change in my routine, but it was worth it to me to have the hair that I wanted.

So you see, change is almost always hard, but some things make it easier to deal with. Or sometimes I surprise myself (and everyone around me!) by suddenly wanting a change.

Spring, 2012

My Asperger's Symptoms

March 2, 2012 at 11:20 AM

When I was first diagnosed with Asperger's, my mom gave me a copy of pages from a book called "School Success For Kids With Asperger's Syndrome." She copied the chapter 'Recognizing and diagnosing AS.' In fact, she made several copies. Then, what I did, was look through the list of symptoms, and I highlighted the ones that applied to me. I even starred the ones that REALLY fit me. Then, when I went to try out college, I gave a highlighted copy to each of my teachers, and explained it all. I think it didn't help much back THEN, because the teachers didn't understand it as well (and some didn't care). But it helps me much more NOW, because I can look over it, and remind myself that some of my traits are Asperger's related. I can also see how I've changed from the highlighted symptoms.

In looking over that list from the book, the top 6 symptoms that I marked with stars were:

- Non-stop worrying about doing well and being well thought of, even with plenty of praise and recognition
- VERY hypersensitive
- Mentally "Shutting down" when I'm overwhelmed
- Having a meltdown when I get overwhelmed or confused and can't get the help I need

- Extreme focus to detail, especially visually
- Not knowing when a task is finished, and being a perfectionist to be sure that I do it right as a result.

So those are my BIG symptoms that stood out to me (and for the most part, still apply today). If you have a chance, I recommend that you pick up this book, and look through the chapter. I had highlighted MANY more symptoms, but those 6 were the ones that I had starred.

Nonverbal Meltdowns

March 3, 2012 at 5:25 PM

Now, I will say right off the bat: I am NOT a non-verbal person. I could probably talk your ear off. That being said, I feel I need to speak up about something that seems to affect non-verbal people with Asperger's or autism. I know that I CAN speak, but that doesn't make communication EASY for me. I still get very frustrated and have the occasional meltdown due to the struggle with communicating with others. That being said, I can't IMAGINE how frustrating it must be to struggle SO MUCH with communication, that you are not even able to speak. It didn't surprise me when someone told me their non-verbal child had meltdowns with no "obvious" cause. Yet to me, the "obvious" cause for a meltdown would be the fact that the child is non-verbal. I mean, how FRUSTRATING it must be to want to communicate SO BADLY with someone, yet be unable to find a way to do so. I would be having meltdowns 24/7.

Like I said, I'm not a non-verbal person, but I can try to put myself in their shoes to try and explain why they may have a seemingly random meltdown.

Meltdowns Verses Tantrums

March 4, 2012 at 9:50 AM

I want to mention that for me, a meltdown and a tantrum are two COMPLETELY different things in my Asperger's vocabulary.

My definition of a meltdown is basically when I get to a point that I just can't HANDLE anymore. It's NOT something I WANT to do, it's not something I do on purpose. Meltdowns are NO FUN, and when they happen, I need my time and space. Some signs that a meltdown may be about to happen for me are: a high-pitched voice, hyperventilation (a panic attack), attempts to leave the situation, and a VERY short temper. Also, I will apologize for my behavior afterwards, but I wish this wasn't necessary for me to do, because it's not as though I can CONTROL my meltdowns very easily.

TANTRUMS on the other hand, are just bad behavior done purposefully. I do have tantrums, but I will usually come back and apologize for my behavior. (Sometimes when I'm still in the MIDDLE of the tantrum.)

So I think the MAIN differences are in the amount of control that I have of the behavior, and the REASON behind it.

Meltdowns: Almost NO control, caused by a situation that I can't handle any more.

Tantrums: Much more control, usually caused by not having something that I want, (not necessarily need).

Autism or Asperger's Is GOOD for Work!

March 5, 2012 at 10:45 AM

I think having Asperger's has been helpful at work, even though it prevents me from working for a long stretch of time. Yes, I can only work part time, but I could work TWO part time shifts, eventually. It's all about taking it slow at first, and building up to the full potential (which, by the way, is AMAZING).

I started my job about 6 or 7 months ago. Yes, I started out very slow. It took me 3 or sometimes 4 hours to complete my work. (Which is actually stretching my limit of how long I can work at one time.) I needed a job coach with me nearly every day, and asked a TON of questions.

However, I started to get the hang of this. Yes, I made plenty of mistakes, and I corrected them. But I found ways to work past the barriers. Now, I am completing my work in about half the time. This is because I know what I'm doing, and I have a routine down. I hardly need my job coach anymore (except for some social situations). I'm also doing MORE than I was before, because I'm getting done so quickly.

So you see, when given the time and a good chance, you will realize just how beneficial someone with autism or Asperger's can be for work. Which BEGS me to ask the question:

Why are so many employers BLIND to this logic? Why are SO MANY people with autism and Asperger's unemployed?

Oh, and I want to thank the people at my job for being so awesome and understanding, and actually giving me this chance. It's working.

Why Time Is So Important

March 5, 2012 at 8:50 PM

The concept of time is really important to me. Whenever my parents go out somewhere, I always ask, "When do you think you will be back?" If they say that they don't know, then I help them out by asking, "Well, are we talking 30 minutes or 3 hours?" I usually get a better idea after that.

Time is important because it gives me a sense of calm and control over my life. I know that if my parents are going to be out for only 30 minutes, I don't want to leave the house because it may be my only quiet time that I get for a while. But if they will be gone for hours, I can go out and STILL have quiet time. Or I know if I need to leave a note about where I will be, or if they won't even be home to read it by the time I'm back.

It also helps me to know how long things take, so that I can prepare myself. Such as how long a drive will take to get where. Should I bring my MP3 player? Will I even have a chance to listen to it? Should I make sure to charge my cell phone so I have a full battery? Do I need to get something done before I leave so I don't have to worry about being too tired to do it later?

Time answers all of those questions and more. It helps me to get the most out of my day, which I have to plan carefully in order to make it through without getting too overwhelmed and having a meltdown.

Off Days

March 7, 2012 at 12:25 AM

I have a lot of wonderful days. However, there are some days where I am "off." I'm not particularly happy, and I'm not completely sad (although, usually by the end of the day, I'm a little depressed). I don't know what causes it, and I don't know how to make it go away. It can happen for a few minutes, or a few days. (Sometimes, even a week.)

Here are a few of the clues that I'm having an off day:

- I'm REALLY hypersensitive to everything
- I'm not making conversation as well as I usually do
- I am easily annoyed
- I'm spending a lot of time alone
- I don't do things very well
- I'm easily overwhelmed.

The truth is, when I'm having an off day, it may SEEM like I don't want to do anything, but I DO want to take part in specific activities. If I take part in something, it's probably an attempt to make contact with the world again, and get me out of this funk. And it's really hard when people don't respond to that attempt. (And I mean REALLY respond.)

I don't want it to sound like it's everyone else's fault. What I'm trying to say is: something is making me feel "off" and that's where others can help. I just need an extra boost of "Hey, we miss you and are thinking of you."

A Question of When or the Last Minute

March 7, 2012 at 6:55 PM

My parents are always telling me that I should let them know when I need something, BEFORE it comes to the last minute. And I always try to do this. However, I have a big problem with it. It's not because I forget, (although, sometimes I DO). It's not because I'm lazy (yes, sometimes I AM). Usually, I have a problem with asking for what I need because I don't know WHEN to ask.

I Have Asperger's

I don't want to ask too many times. I don't want them to forget. I don't want to stress them out. I don't want to bombard them when they first walk in the door, or when they are about to leave. I don't want to ask them when they are mad, or busy, or about to go to bed, or have just woken up. I can't ask them when they are on the phone, or when they are cooking, or watching TV, or working, or doing taxes or paying bills.

So I know when NOT to ask them, but I don't know the right time when I SHOULD ask them. Because after all of this, I'm waiting and waiting and preparing myself for that perfect moment, and I just can't seem to get it right. So, in the end, it ALWAYS comes down to the last minute. Which I know is ALSO a bad time. So maybe, if I had a list of GOOD times, it would be easier for me to ask them about things.

And this rule doesn't JUST apply to my parents. It applies to EVERYONE. Tell me when I CAN do things, and I will try to plan it into MY day. Otherwise, it won't happen.

Self-Esteem

March 8, 2012 at 11:20 AM

I have Asperger's. I'm not dumb. I'm not "bad." I work every day to make sure I'm seen as the person who I want to be: myself. I don't understand what the big idea is about being "labeled." It's kind of like saying that someone has blue eyes. Great!

But what's behind those eyes? What kind of person are you? Are you kind? Are you polite? Are you trustworthy? These are all what matter to me. You could be the most "popular" person, but if you are just plain rude, you will have lost my respect.

I never really cared about being popular, because those people were usually mean to me. I know what is right, and I know who I want to be. I wanted to be respected for the RIGHT reasons, not for some lie I told that I didn't believe in.

So, forget "normal," whatever normal is. I've always been drawn towards the "weird" and "crazy" things. I take it as a compliment when people call me that! I would much rather stand out as myself than blend in with everyone else. The truth is, I think the more people are happy with themselves, the cooler they are.

To Tell or Not To Tell

March 10, 2012 at 7:10 PM

Disclosing information about oneself is a completely personal choice. For me, talking about my Asperger's really is usually no big deal. In fact, I LOVE to educate others! If talking about myself helps someone else, then I will explode with whatever information people want.

The only time I usually don't want to tell someone is if they will judge me on it. I don't mean the kind of judging as in, "Ew, you have Asperger's? You're WEIRD!" I actually mean the "What? Asperger's? Really? Ok, do you want a free pass?"

For instance, at my piano festival today (which went very well, as far as I can tell)… I wasn't GOING to tell the judge that I have Asperger's, because I didn't want an "easy A" so to speak. What ended up making me decide to tell the judge was that I realized that

I Have Asperger's

I may say something rude without knowing. I didn't want THAT to hurt my score. It's the stuff that I don't even understand would be a problem that I want a "free pass" for. But I didn't need to tell that judge that I have Asperger's because I play piano any worse, or to "impress" her. I just didn't want to be seen as rude.

The truth is, most of the time, someone telling me that I'm weird or crazy is an awesome compliment. Who wants to be just like everyone else? Again, I also enjoy educating others.

However, using the "Asperger's Card" to get the easy way out? I really try not to do that.

I Have Asperger's!

March 11, 2012 at 12:15 AM

When I was younger, I never understood why people were upset when I asked if I could help. I thought that a rule should NEVER be broken, no matter what. I wondered why people were crying when someone I didn't even know had passed away. I was SO confused by the homework questions that asked me why the character in the book we were reading said a certain line. I remember walking around giving people "the middle finger," asking them why it was so bad because, after all, it is JUST a finger. I remember being confused as to why my Dad said it was "dark" outside, when I could still see PLENTY. There was a time that I laughed when I threw a softball to my friend, and it came so close to her head that it knocked out an earring. I wasn't trying to be mean when I laughed. I just didn't realize that I had nearly knocked her unconscious.

Erin Clemens

I started my first self-stimming when I was 3 months old: banging my head against my pillow to get to sleep.

I have Asperger's. I can drive. I can carry out mostly decent conversations. I even have a job that I LOVE, working with animals.

It may seem to many people that I DON'T have Asperger's. These people didn't see me when I nearly dropped out of school because I was SO overwhelmed and over-stimulated. They didn't see me struggling not to kill myself because I felt SO stood. They didn't see the meltdowns over school or chores or any of that. They didn't see the year my parents refused to let me learn how to drive because I wasn't ready. They didn't see the first 3 or 4 jobs that I DIDN'T get because I was too slow. All they see is a "normal" 22-year-old girl. It hurts.

I have Asperger's. I was ALMOST diagnosed in 2001, and it was dismissed because I was so social. I was officially diagnosed by a doctor who did a neuropsychological evaluation, when I started having panic attacks daily in 2005. I don't want to have to prove that I have it anymore. I want to be trusted and not have to pull out the boxes upon BOXES of paperwork my Mom has gone through to make sure that I get the help that I need to make the amazing progress that I am making.

I have Asperger's.

Blowing Bubbles
March 13, 2012 at 8:50 PM

I love blowing bubbles. I love the free spirited nature of it. I love how it makes me feel like a kid again. I love how simple it is, yet how much it's fascinating. I love seeing the look on little kids' faces when they see the bubbles. I also love, how, for some strange reason, it's one of the only "kids' toys" that I can play with without seeming weird. I will never understand why playing with simple toys is supposed to be only for kids. I mean, do you ever see an adult playing with, say, a doll or building blocks - without a kid?

Something about bubbles just makes everything seem OK in the world. It's ok to make a small mess. It's ok if they pop. It's ok if you can't make a perfect bubble. It's even ok where the bubbles go. Over the house? Into the neighbor's yard? On the car? On yourself?

Bubbles always seem to make me smile, and appreciate life a little bit more, and the simple things in it.

Is Autistic The New R Word?

March 14, 2012 at 8:55 PM

As a person with Asperger's, I have never liked hearing the "R" word. (For those of you unfamiliar with it, the "R" word is the word "retarded" or "retard" used to insult someone.) I made sure that I told people how much it offended me if they said it. I asked them to find a better word to use. Many of my friends have been respectful and don't use it. It has always sickened me to hear it slowly catching on as being a popular word.

I have heard the R word being used on TV, in movies, and sadly, I have even seen it in print. Sometimes, I just let it go, because I could see it catching on so quickly, and I feel so helpless to try and stop it.

Then I saw a trailer for a movie the other day. The movie is supposed to be a comedy about two "dumb" guys. In the trailer, there were two guys who had made this big chart on a cork board to try to explain their situation. (Similar to what Temple Grandin was seen doing in her movie.) The man listening to the guys shakes his head, and says "What are you guys, autistic?" Then, as if trying to HIDE the joke, the guys reply "Well, yes, we are *artistic.*"

I have never been SO offended in my life. How could the actor agree to say the line, the writers be ok with writing the line, the producers be ok with producing the movie, and any theater agree to show something so awful. I'm very scared that "Autistic" is becoming the new R-word. It just shows me how ignorant and messed up some people are in this world.

The Funny Thing With Friends

March 17, 2012 at 7:35 AM

It seems to me that every time I begin hating a person, and I mean for a silly reason, I will end up being best friends with them in the end. This has happened to me with at least two people in life (that I can remember so far).

The first one was this know-it-all kid. She was a teacher's pet, she could do more than I could, and she was just so annoying. Then one day, I sat in a squeaky desk. Of COURSE, she did, too. I started to wiggle back and forth in my desk to make it louder than hers. She thought it was funny, and started doing the same. I just couldn't win. Even her DESK was squeakier than mine. Suddenly, we both started laughing. We moved our desks next to each other, and became best friends. She taught me a lot over the years, and then, ironically, I started teaching her things. I taught her about Asperger's and autism and animals and more. I finally realized that our friendship was more important than who was smarter. (Or who had the squeakiest desk!)

The other person I can remember was a teacher of mine. The moment I walked into the classroom, I thought "Ugh, this teacher is trying to be cool." (I hated when teachers thought they could be like kids by acting or talking like them.) Another thing I couldn't stand was that this teacher cursed. (I was strict with my "no cursing" rule at the time.) I forget what else I didn't like, but for some reason my mom remembers that I said I hated this teacher from day one. This teacher ended up being my favorite one in my entire life. This person didn't act like a kid to try to relate to them. They actually DO relate to them. They understood me better than anyone else at school. I forget when I started to actually befriend them, but somehow I did, and GOSH am I glad. Never have I had a better teacher.

And the really funny thing, is that, some of the people who I started out absolutely LOVING, I've ended up moving on from. (Not EVERYONE fits into these love/hate categories.) I guess the main idea is that I know some REALLY great people. And first impressions are not always the last!

Dear Ellen DeGeneres

March 18, 2012 at 7:50 PM

Dear Ellen DeGeneres,

Hi there! I am a 22-year-old girl with Asperger's Syndrome. Asperger's Syndrome is on the autism spectrum. I absolutely LOVE your show. On Twitter, my friend @GretchenLeary and myself (@AspergerSadie) have been trying to contact you to ask you if you would do another show on autism and Asperger's. The spectrum has a big range, and we feel that you would be perfect to help us educate people about it.

April is Autism Awareness month. Would you be willing to plan a show (I don't know how far in advance you plan them) to spread some awareness? It would mean so much to my friend and I, and everyone else on the autism spectrum.

I understand how very busy you must be. Thank you so much for taking the time to read this.

Sincerely,

Admin of www.ihaveaspergers.webs.com

Twitter: @AspergerSadie

Youtube: keyword erinclem

(http://www.youtube.com/user/erinclem)

To Whom It May Concern
March 18, 2012 at 10:55 PM

To Whom It May Concern,

The autism community needs your help for Autism Awareness Month!

I have Asperger's Syndrome which is on the autism spectrum, and I am asking, if for nothing else, for you to listen. If you listen, then the world may as well.

The autism community needs your help. So much more awareness is desperately needed. We need you to speak for those who cannot speak and those whose words are often dismissed, mocked, or even used against them.

Would you have Dani Bowman appear on your show to promote autism/Asperger's Syndrome Awareness for Autism Awareness Month? She is an incredible advocate.

Sincerely,

Admin of www.ihaveaspergers.webs.com

Twitter: @AspergerSadie

Youtube: keyword erinclem

(http://www.youtube.com/user/erinclem)

Blow Bubbles For Autism

March 20, 2012 at 5:50 PM

I absolutely LOVE bubbles. They're fun and they bring joy to people. So I was SUPER excited when I heard that Thursday, April 26th is Blow Bubbles For Autism Day! I just think this is the best idea in the world. Spreading awareness for autism and Asperger's through one of my favorite activities! Join me in spirit on Thursday, April 26, 2012. Blow them for yourself, someone you love, someone you know, or someone you don't know. Just blow them and watch them float away with your troubles and frustration and anger and sorrow.

High Pain Tolerance

March 23, 2012 at 10:25 AM

I've noticed that I, along with other people on the autism spectrum, tend to have a higher pain tolerance. I don't know if this is common for ALL people with ASD, but situations have suggested it to me. Here are a few of them:

1. A friend had an ear infection, but didn't even feel it until their ear-drum was about to burst. Then they barely felt a little bit of pain. (Their ear was treated and is better now.)

2. A friend had a broken bone (can't remember if it was a collar bone, an arm, or an ankle) and went for days without ing. They finally went to the doctor when there were visual signs of something major going on.

3. A friend had a broken finger, but thought they had just jammed it. They finally went to the doctor when the finger began to swell too much.

I don't know WHY these extreme cases have occurred, but here is my theory:

Our nervous system is SO sensitive, that we are actually USED to the pain. Or perhaps we can't tell the difference between major and minor pain. When we hear a loud noise, it hurts, but we know we have to deal with it. When we have a terrible ear infection, it hurts, but we don't realize that it's an ear infection, so we figure we have to deal with it.

Whatever the reason, it's an interesting trait.

Happy Friday!

March 23, 2012 at 6:35 PM

I had such an amazing day today. First, I got things done at work well. Then I finally was able to budget my money on my own, with plenty of money to spare! Next, I celebrated this with the perfect ice cream sundae. After that, I tried on a bathing suit, and it fit perfectly the very first time! Then I ran into a friend while I was shopping, and enjoyed talking with them. Next I got some fresh fruit, and made a delicious smoothie! I also went to the park and blew bubbles for the kids on the perfect day, and even got a compliment from a parent telling me how well I work with kids. After that, I dusted a little in my room, and finally won two games of "Sorry!" Oh, I also got to talk with a friend online that moved away, plus I got to pet-sit by watching TV, surfing the web, and playing piano in the house with the dog. Yes, today has been a GREAT, happy, Friday!

Getting To Know People

March 24, 2012 at 10:40 AM

I don't know how long it takes to become an acquaintance. I don't know how long it takes to become friends. I don't know how long it takes to become REALLY GOOD friends. I have Asperger's.

When I was in 6th grade (about 12 years old), I took a picture of someone I knew from my yearbook, and put it in my locker. This person's "best friend" became very upset. I couldn't understand why. It's still hard to understand completely, but I now have the idea that it's not okay.

It takes about a year for me to fully feel comfortable with someone. Once I'm comfortable, I feel like I'm welcome to do whatever I please. I know it's not always true, but I hope that my friendship will save any miss-communication that I happen to have.

It's hard to fully understand relationships. It's probably why I'm single, and absolutely loving it. (I have enough to take care of for myself!) So, sorry guys and gals, but I'm not available! I am, however, open to being a great friend!

Autism Awareness Is Hard Work!

March 25, 2012 at 5:50 PM

When I saw my friend from Twitter asking Ellen DeGeneres to do another show about autism and Asperger's awareness, I jumped on the idea with her! Of course! Ask someone to help spread awareness; someone we love and we think would care. I didn't really think it would get very far, but hey, I'd rather do something than nothing.

Soon, people started to re-tweet our request to Ellen to do a show. That's when I thought: Hey, she's onto something! This could truly work, but EVERYONE needs to be in it together.

Day one went well. Day two a little less, and by the time we were at day seventeen, things started looking grim. Only a few WONDERFUL tweeters were re-tweeting, and we still have had no response. Both my friend and I have started to get really depressed and wonder if this will ever happen. She has put money into the campaign, I have put as much time and effort into it as I can, since I can't afford much advertising.

It's now day eighteen of our thirty day campaign. It's March 25, 2012. What I am now asking is for anyone to please help us. WE are NOT trying to get onto the show. What we are asking at this point is for any show host to do an entire show on autism and Asperger's.

Looking Back:

While we never got a response from Ellen DeGeneres, I'm still grateful for the work we did on this campaign. Not only did it spread a lot of awareness about autism, but it really brought my friend and I closer together.

Happy World Autism Awareness Day!

April 2, 2012 at 10:20 AM

One of my favorite days has come again! It's World Autism Awareness Day! (April 2) If you are having trouble figuring out how to support or spread awareness for people on the autism spectrum, here are a couple of ideas:

Buy an autism awareness item. (I recommend my Autism Awareness Duct Tape Bracelets! Money goes to help others on the autism spectrum!)

Wear blue! The color blue seems to be what everyone has decided is the color for autism awareness.

Light up your house blue!

Attend an autism awareness event in your area!

Above all, remember to accept and work on better understanding those on the autism spectrum.

Happy World Autism Awareness Day everyone!

A Post For My Members

April 4, 2012 at 5:55 PM

This is a special post for my current, future, or even past members. (It's not as good as the one I just wrote that was deleted by mistake, but it will do.)

It's been about a year since this website first went up. It is still up, and for that I'm so happy! I'm glad I can help to spread so much awareness about autism and Asperger's. However, I'm not the only one who has worked into making *I Have Asperger's* the website it is today. Lots of family, friends, and people whom I've never even met have helped to make this site possible.

I want to thank you all for showing me such support. What is one thing that you would like this website to have? Is it forums? Instant messaging and chat? (These are pretty much the only two apps I can get.) Or do you have another suggestion?

Please note, I tried the forums on this site once before, and they were abused by advertising from members. I can try it again, and we can see what happens.

Please leave your comments and suggestions below!

Depression
April 11, 2012 at 9:40 AM

Yes, I have Asperger's. I also have depression. They are two separate things. I see my Asperger's as being something that I can work with and it can be positive. With depression, I honestly don't see the "good" of it.

Depression is one of those things that can make you feel like you are the only person on the planet when you're in the middle of a crowd of friends. It's hard because you can see yourself bringing other people down with you. It's annoying because you cry for no reason, and BECAUSE there's no specific reason that you're crying, there's nothing that can make you feel better. You just have to wait it out, and follow doctor's orders. It's even harder, because while you WANT to get better, you lack motivation to TRY to get better. In the end, it feels like a downwards spiral.

So, I'm writing this post to explain any lack of blog posts lately. I think depression also takes away from the quality of my writing. Sorry about that.

Peace

April 13, 2012 at 6:15 PM

I went to an awards breakfast today. (I didn't win, but I was nominated. This nomination earned me a free pass to a flower and garden show.) Everyone was so nice to me there. They knew I had Asperger's, so they seated me close to a door so I had less of a chance of feeling overwhelmed in a crowd of over 200 people. It really helped. I still ended up using my sunglasses to feel less anxious, and ear plugs to lessen the noise.

Anyways, the breakfast was nice, and when it was over, I got to see the gardens. But I think my favorite part WASN'T the gardens. It was a special meadow/field that they had. It was so empty and open and quiet. SO quiet. I remember walking through that field, and I was the ONLY one there. All around me was grass, and trees in the distance. At one point, I just stopped smack dab in the middle of it all, and looked around soaking it up. No cars, no people, no evidence of major civilization. There was a groundhog that ran by, a few birds flew around me, and that was about it. A thought crossed my mind: "Is this EARTH?" It seems like a silly question, but if you think about it you'll understand why I would ask that to myself. I've grown up, without EVER having gone camping, or anywhere by myself in the middle of nothing. No litter, no electricity, no pollution, no noise. And when you have Asperger's, this all plays a BIG role in life. You can smell the pollution, you can hear everything. I've NEVER heard anything that quiet in my entire life.

It's funny, because I'm not a HUGE nature person, not that I have anything against it, I'm just not THAT into it. But that meadow was the most beautiful place I have ever been. (Minus the goose poo in the grass!)

Understanding Fears or Common Sense

April 22, 2012 at 9:35 AM

I learned something new the other day. There are rational and irrational fears. I mean, I KNEW this, but the problem was, I didn't know the difference. Let me explain.

I have had a fear of bees for a long time. When I was about 20 years old, my fear had turned into a full blown phobia, where I didn't feel safe under the covers of my own bed. I went to get help, and found a great person who helped me to overcome my fear. (Well, for the most part.) Basically, I had exposure therapy to slowly get used to bees. If I was just a little scared, I needed to try and handle it. Like I said, this all worked, so I have been pretty happy for the past year or two.

Now, here comes the problem:

At my work, there was a bees' nest outside. Most people may automatically think, "Okay, so, call the boss and tell them there's a problem that makes it unsafe to work." However, I felt my fear of bees taking over, and I thought it was my phobia returning. I thought "I have to try to handle this, because I'm a little scared." I tried to work through this group of about 10 bees, but I couldn't. I was so devastated, thinking that I would have to quit my job because I was too scared to work, I was in tears. Finally, I asked the person who had helped me with my fear to help me again. I was slightly surprised and VERY relieved to hear that I should tell my boss about the nest, because it might be unsafe. I called up by boss and explained the situation, and they helped me to figure out the best, SAFE way to get the job done. I admitted that I used to have a phobia about bees, and my boss jokingly replied, "Yeah, and now it's common sense!"

What's funny is that I didn't know it was common sense. At least, not right away. I'm so used to it being ME who has to deal with things, that I couldn't see when I DIDN'T have to deal. I'm so used to having an irrational fear of bees, that I didn't recognize my body's (probably instinctive!) RATIONAL fear of a bees' NEST.

Now I know why I need people to support and coach me through things. It's because sometimes, I really, truly just don't comprehend. And if it were anyone else in my shoes, I would have told them it was an unsafe situation. I have common sense, sometimes I just don't understand it. (Try making sense of THAT statement!)

Autism and Asperger's Stereotypes

April 28, 2012 at 6:20 PM

I'm writing this one because I've finally realized, people don't understand me. I mean, I've always KNOWN this, but I didn't realize that some aren't even OPEN to understanding me. Below, I'm going to write a small list of traits some people may think of when they want to describe autism or Asperger's:

- Awkward
- Anti-social
- Savant
- Expert in Math or Science
- No Eye-contact
- Tantrums
- Unimaginative
- Rocking
- Flapping
- Obsessions
- Dumb
- Not good with communication
- Rain Man

There are LOTS of traits people think of when they describe autism or Asperger's. The thing is, what I listed above is mostly stereotypical. Here are some traits I personally like to think of:

- Creative
- Fun
- Unique
- Hard-working
- Misunderstood

Yes, misunderstood. Some people DO have the traits from the first list. But, just like any random person off the street, people on the spectrum are unique individuals who will have varying traits from focused hobbies to a million interests! So the next time you say "but you don't SEEM like you have Asperger's," I promise you I will ask "Oh, really? What does Asperger's look like to you?" Because maybe then, I can teach someone something new about autism.

I Have Asperger's to "I Wish I Didn't Have Asperger's": #AutismPositivity2012

April 29, 2012 at 10:30 PM

Author's Note: In 2012, someone did a search for Asperger's and came up with the result of a blog post that read "I wish I didn't have Asperger's." This started a buzz all over social media, and it was requested that people write a blog post in response to this person's statement. Our goal was to give the person hope and change their perspective about having Asperger's. The following is my post.

Dear "I Wish I Didn't Have Asperger's",

I'm SO sorry that you feel this way. I don't know what caused these feelings to come about, but I can promise you that you don't have to be alone. Many people go through teasing, or misunderstanding, or downright discrimination. It's not RIGHT, but it's true. I am here to say: I am with you in your struggle, but I am also with you in the triumph.

Yes, the triumph. The beauty of being different from many others. The glory of knowing that YOU are not just "anyone." The obstacles that you overcome have not just the badge of "well done" waiting at the end, but you can also know that you overcome them AND you have Asperger's. YOU have talents that many others do not. Above all, YOU are so important, because YOU are here, and if it weren't for your Asperger's, you would be MUCH different, and therefore, NOT you.

So please, take a moment to remember, that yes, there is struggle and injustice and downright failure, but you are still human. Asperger's will NEVER take that away from you. But you can decide to take away the wonderful qualities associated with Asperger's. The qualities such as being unique, intelligent, fun, caring, and more.

I am sorry that you wish you didn't have Asperger's, but I am not sorry that I have Asperger's. I hope you can join me in what will be a new, positive feeling for you.

Sincerely,

Admin of *I Have Asperger's*

www.ihaveaspergers.webs.com

@AspergerSadie

Does Asperger's Make You Lazy?

April 30, 2012 at 10:50 PM

I saw this question in the search options, and I decided that I'd better take a moment to answer it for people. So if you've found yourself on this page by searching this, I hope that you'll understand the following.

I have Asperger's. I can also be lazy sometimes. However, these two traits are COMPLETELY unrelated. My household dictionary describes the term "lazy" as being "Unwilling to work." However, with Asperger's, it's not about being unWILLING to work, but unABLE. I can get to a point where I am so overwhelmed, overstimulated, exhausted, distraught- you name it, that I'm at a point where I'm not CAPABLE of working. No matter how much I WANT to, or TRY to, I will have a meltdown because my body and mind cannot continue.

Compare it to speeding down the highway while it's pouring rain, the windshield wipers don't work, you can't pull over, the radio is at full blast because it's broken, there is a siren coming up from somewhere behind you, and you have a passenger asking you to answer an algebra question. Are you unWILLING to answer the algebra problem, or are you unABLE to? Can you think about algebra in this situation? Not really. Are you lazy in this situation? Absolutely not.

Don't get me wrong, I am human. Therefore, I am lazy every so often. Yes, there are many times I don't want to get up in the morning. I don't always feel like practicing my piano. And to be honest, who really WANTS to do chores?

But please understand, there is a difference between the not WANTING and the not being ABLE.

No, Asperger's does NOT make you lazy. It seems to do the opposite, in fact. I WANT to be able to do so much more sometimes, but I'm not always ABLE to. So I do the best I can. (And honestly, that's a LOT!)

Moving Out In 90 Days With Asperger's

May 1, 2012 at 10:40 AM

I've been trying to find a way to move out for a while now. In doing so, my parents and I have decided that I need to try to be out in 90 days, for everyone's sake. We just need space from each other, and it's about time for me to get out on my own. As with any young adult, I'm going to be facing my challenges of ing. What makes this goal even more interesting is the fact that I have Asperger's.

So, I've decided that I'm going to do a series of videos on YouTube. I will post a video each week on the progress I've made, the obstacles I've faced, and ultimately, my journey towards moving out.

A Moment

May 5, 2012 at 12:30 AM

Please just take a moment to read this.

I know that it's not even close to September as I write this, but I want to say something about September 11, 2001. As terrible as it was, and NO ONE deserved to die for what I'm about to say happened, take a moment to watch videos about what happened AFTER that day. I see the horror, but then I see people stopping to help each other. I see love and care and so much PEACE. I see such amazing things that only seem to happen when there are tragedies like this. It saddens me that only the worst things in life can bring out the best in some people. And like I said, NO ONE deserves to die for these wonderful acts of love and kindness. So why do we wait?

Talking Is The Easy Part

May 15, 2012 at 4:55 PM

I've had many people say to me, "You're so brave for sharing such personal information with everyone." I suppose that's a compliment, and I appreciate that. What confuses me is this: I don't FEEL any NEED to be brave. It's not scary for me. It's not embarrassing, or shameful, or any of that. Not that I don't feel that at other times (I have my share of secrets, too!), but speaking out about autism and Asperger's is easy for me. The difficult part is getting people to listen.

When I was in school, before I was even diagnosed, I tried to ask for help. Most people just said "You're doing fine," and moved on. This was where I started to REALLY struggle. It was hard for me to ask for help, and to hear someone say that I don't even need help was SO frustrating. After a few years, I realized I had to speak up for myself. I got to a point where I was so frustrated I wouldn't allow myself to be ignored anymore. If I needed help, well then gosh darn-it, I needed help!

This is why I always tell people who ask me if I'm open to speaking about my life that I'm more than happy to do so AS LONG AS PEOPLE ARE WILLING TO LISTEN. One of my biggest fears is speaking to a crowd of people who either talk over me or show other signs of being uninterested in what I have to say. It's not a fear of ME making a mistake or anything like that. It's a fear of being misunderstood and ignored.

So In the end, my bravery doesn't come from speaking about what some people consider to be personal issues (and I barely know what is considered to be "personal," or WHY for that matter...). My only bravery is facing the same fear every time I speak: that I will once again be ignored, misunderstood, or doubted. My life is pretty much an open book for hundreds or thousands of people to learn from. (Granted, it's what my parents are willing to share, too.) What's there to be embarrassed of, though, of being a human being?

I'm Like You, But Different

May 17, 2012 at 4:00 PM

I've heard a lot of people say "You don't seem like you have Asperger's." When this happens, I will either reply with "What is Asperger's supposed to look like?" or, if I'm feeling lazy, I say "I know." When I tell people the things that bother me, like certain sounds (lawn mowers and chain saws or weed-whackers) people will say, "Lots of people don't like those sounds." As if they are trying to say that I'm so called "normal" and that many people feel the same way I do about things. But they don't understand.

I Have Asperger's

When I say that the sound of a weed-whacker bothers me, I don't mean that it's just something that annoys me, like many people feel. What I mean is that if I don't close the windows, turn on my sound soother, listen to music, or somehow get AWAY from that noise, my stress level will go through the roof and I will be ten times more likely to have a meltdown. I have yet to see someone who doesn't have Asperger's shut the window on a beautiful day JUST because of the sound of a weed-whacker down the street, let alone have a meltdown if they DON'T shut the window.

So yes, in some ways, I am like other people. In fact, in many ways, OTHER PEOPLE are LIKE ME! However, it's the idea of how severely the situations affect me that differs from how they affect many neurotypical people.

Looking Back:
Now when people say, "But you don't seem like you have Asperger's," I like to respond with, "Yes I do!"

Happy Birthday To Me! (I'm 23!)
May 29, 2012 at 8:55 PM

Today is my birthday, and I've decided to take a moment to enjoy it before it comes to an end. (Not that I haven't enjoyed it already!) I got a balloon and some presents and cards, and it's been great! Of course, nothing could top my two biggest birthday wishes. My two biggest birthday wishes were:

1) For my dog to still be around to "sing" (bark) the song Happy Birthday. (She does this for everyone on their birthday, and she

usually starts it off, too!) We have been concerned lately, because of her torn ACL injury, and her not being able to handle the surgery to fix it. (She's 12.)

2) For me to move out!

I'm very happy to report that BOTH of my biggest birthday wishes have come true!!!!! 😁

........."and many moooooore!" (BARK!)

Am I Really THAT Rude?
May 30, 2012 at 4:05 PM

I've heard of the stereotype that lots of people with Asperger's tend to be rude. Yes, that may be true in some aspects. I'm not GREAT at social situations, and I often find myself clueless as to why my parents are SO upset when I say something a certain way. I don't always remember to write thank-you cards, and I don't always ask others how they are doing.

HOWEVER

I DO say please and thank you, (out of pure reflex!). I DO hold doors for people, and apologize if I find out I HAVE been rude. I don't curse (at other people, or when it's inappropriate), I don't put others down, and I try to basically treat others the way I would want to be treated.

I honestly feel that I am more consciously polite than most people. I feel so many people are unaware of their disrespectful behaviors, and sometimes this frustrates me. Just recently, there was an incident where I felt I was the only person of about forty who could respect the people involved while still stating my honest opinion. In the end, I was thankful for help I received, and apologized for any inconvenience I caused. But I was patient, I didn't shout, I didn't accuse anyone of anything, and I was just downright respectful. I cannot say much of the same for the rest of the people involved. That saddens me, and frustrates me that I'm seen as one of those kinds of people.

People argue, people threaten, people accuse and deny. People complain, people attack, you name it. And I'm not going to sit here and say that I'm perfect, because I'm anything BUT. However, I thank my parents for raising me to be a conscious mature, polite, respectful person. If I'm ever extremely rude, it's most likely because I'm oblivious to it, but I would never WANT to be, or do it on purpose.

Summer & Fall, 2012

Feeling Disoriented
June 3, 2012 at 10:45 AM

I just recently moved out of my parents' house and into my own place. I love being on my own, not having to worry about people telling me what to do. It's a great sense of freedom. The trouble is, I feel like I have too much freedom. I don't know what to DO with myself. Plus, I haven't gotten into a routine yet. When I have a routine, I can work around it, and I spend less time THINKING and more time just DOING. Now, I have to think about EVERY little detail. When will I run an errand? What do I need to do before I leave? Am I forgetting anything? How can I save gas on this trip? Do I need anything else while I'm out? How long will this take me? Do I need to call anyone about anything first? Do I have the money to buy things or should I wait? How long CAN I wait before I NEED to buy it? What do I need for tomorrow? Should I get that now, or later on?

All of these questions spin around my head because I have not settled into a true routine yet. The simple things seem like they are the most complicated, and complicated things are out of the question. I just don't quite know where I belong at the moment.

May My Dog Rest In Peace

June 6, 2012 at 9:35 AM

I'm very sad to say that we had to put our dog down yesterday.

She was an amazing dog. She was born on October 5, 1999.

I remember the way that we threw her toys, and she would chase after them, slide on the hardwood floor, bounce into the wall, pick up the toy, run and then slide back again to us. What a puppy she was! Squeaker toys never lasted more than a day. The toy would last, but the squeaker would be broken! Of course, her FAVORITE toy was her red treat ball. It took her at most a few minutes to get the treats out of that ball. We would hide it for her, and then she would go and search for it. For her very first Easter, we placed a few treats in a plastic egg, and she saw it, picked up the egg, dropped it so it would crack open, ate the treats and left the egg. She loved getting the paper even though it was so heavy it would often slip out of the plastic and fall all over the yard. She would find my shoes for me, she would wake me up in the morning, she would open and close doors, and so much more. Her favorite thing to do was to chase rabbits. (And eat rabbit poo!)

There are so many wonderful things I remember about this dog. She was there for me during the times I really needed her most. I would not be here if it weren't for her. I feel that God gave me this dog, and yesterday, I gave her back. She was the best gift God could ever give me, and I'm so grateful for that gift. She passed away just days after I moved out.

One of the hardest things for me right now is knowing that I can no longer say that I have a dog.

Good-bye, girl. I love you, Pups. Rest in peace.

Hello?

June 9, 2012 at 9:25 AM

So I've been living on my own for about a week now. I LOVE living on my own, but that doesn't mean I want to be a hermit, which is apparently what everyone ELSE wants to do.

I grew up in a very friendly neighborhood. It was the kind of neighborhood where you were good friends with at least the 5 or 10 houses closest to your own. I could walk outside and there was almost always someone to strike up a conversation with. Almost every yard, even those with fences around them, was considered to be shared, because we were all friends. If someone needed a stick of butter, it's almost safe to say that - even if the neighbors weren't home - you could go in and take a stick of butter and tell them later. It's hard to explain, but we were basically a REALLY tight knit community that looked out for each other not just because it was the right thing to do, but because we WANTED to. We cared about each other, no matter how annoying we might be sometimes. It was RUDE to tell someone that they were bothering you, because we always helped each other the rest of the time. The best part was that we all could pretty much give our talents and services to each other. The computer expert would fix your computer. The electrician would fix the wiring. The chef would cook great food for everyone, and the musician would gladly share some lessons. In return, you would just do the same. I always offered a dog walk here or there, some training, or a quick feeding. If windows were left open before a storm, someone would shut them. If a pet was loose, people were out looking instantly.

This may seem like it's too good to be true. But I promise you, this is how the neighborhood is.

Which is why when I moved to a new place, I was so disappointed. I say hi to someone, and they barely hear me. Nobody really knows anyone. Cell phones and iPods have replaced the conversations. People are so BUSY with themselves that no one seems to actually CARE about anyone else. I've tried to meet and greet people, but it takes two for a conversation.

So what have I been doing? I've been visiting my old neighborhood every day. And they have all told me to come over anytime.

Decisions, Decisions

June 10, 2012 at 9:05 AM

I have so many things I need to do, and plenty of other things that I want to do. The problem with this, for me, is that I can't decide on what to do, or if I should do something else first. Some tasks, such as personal care (bathing, cleaning my apartment, paying bills, etc.) I know I need to keep close tabs on. Other things, however, are long overdue (thank you notes, practicing piano, possibly changing my website SLIGHTLY, calling a friend, and plenty more).

So at this point, I know I have to get certain things done, but I'm feeling the urge to do the things that don't need to be done. Then, I can't decide which less important task to work on. The biggest issue that comes from this type of situation is the fact that by the time I decide on what to do, I've lost interest in it. In the end, I tend to not feel like doing anything, have nothing accomplished, and start to feel overwhelmed. Sometimes, it gets to the point where I shut down completely, and I CAN'T get anything done.

Occasionally, I wonder which part of this vicious cycle is due to the Asperger's, and which part is something that everyone goes through.

More often, however, I wonder how I'm going to break the cycle, or even prevent it in the first place.

Mockingbird: A Book About Asperger's

June 15, 2012 at 11:00 AM

I've decided to go ahead and read my first book about a child with Asperger's. I don't usually like to read books about Asperger's because not only do they make me feel self-conscious, but I feel like I'm reading something I already know. I didn't want to read the book *The Curious Case of The Dog In The Night*, I didn't like the movie *Mozart and the Whale*, and the main reason I liked the movie *Temple Grandin* was because it let others EXPERIENCE what autism is like, from an autistic point of view.

But this book, *Mockingbird* by Kathryn Erskine is a children's book. It's also written from the point of view of a child with Asperger's, though I do believe it's fiction. After skimming the first few pages, I've decided I want to try and read this one. I want to be able to recommend a book for people to read that I can agree with. One written by someone who DOESN'T have Asperger's, but seems to understand what it's like. That's the amazing part. How can someone who doesn't live the diagnosis understand so well? I guess I will have to find out JUST how well this author understands.

I also want to read it, because someone I babysit for owns this book, and also knows I have Asperger's. Maybe I can help this person to understand me even better by discussing this book with them.

How Are You Feeling?

June 18, 2012 at 7:25 PM

Sometimes, I just can't tell how people are feeling. I regularly ask the questions, "Are you bored?" "Are you tired?" "Are you feeling well?" and many more. I don't do it to annoy people, but because I know I can't tell on my own, so I may as well outright ask them.

Just today, I asked someone three questions in a row: "Are you bored?" Answer: "No." "Are you tired?" Answer: "No." These are the two most common ones associated with this person. Finally, I remembered an incident that had occurred earlier that the person had been upset about. This led me to ask, "Are you mad?" Answer: "Yes."

I got it! I was so happy that I had gotten it! But....ok, what's the best way to RESPOND to that?

In the end, I settled on, "I'm sorry about what happened." Even though it wasn't really my fault, I still wanted to make sure they weren't mad at ME for some reason. Of course, they weren't.

I never really thought about how similar any emotions are to each other according to behaviors. I just ask the usual questions, and try to figure out how to deal with the answers that come.

I'm Still Here!

June 30, 2012 at 7:10 PM

I promise I haven't given up on this blog. I've just been SOOO busy lately with work, pet-sitting, cleaning, and taking care of my new fish! It's great to have income, it's just very stressful. So please, bear with me as I settle into my new place, with a new life.

I've don't think I've had ONE day of sleeping-in within the past 4 weeks. I've been working every morning, whether at the kennel or pet-sitting. Lately, we've had more than 5 dogs staying at the kennel!

I'm not complaining, just explaining why I haven't been keeping up with my blog. But I WAS getting really stressed because of a lack of routine. So, I finally got myself a fish. This way, I have someone to talk to and to routinely care for. I feel like I have a reason to wake up other than going to work.

Writer's Block

July 15, 2012 at 7:50 PM

Obviously, this blog post won't be too long, considering the title. It's not so much writer's block as it is depression and anxiety building up lately. I haven't had the energy in me to write. It's not just with writing, though. I haven't had energy to get to places on time, leave my apartment in general, decide on things to do, and just plain focus. I've had insomnia and have been grinding my teeth or tensing my muscles due to stress and anxiety. The hardest part is actually ending this blog post, because I can't think straight!

Things I Remember Most About School

July 18, 2012 at 12:00 AM

- Bells ringing
- Lockers slamming
- Flagpoles clanging
- Kids laughing
- Shoes squeaking
- Shoving/pushing/running/slapping
- Books falling
- High pitched girls talking/screaming
- Whistles blowing
- iPods blaring - music blasting
- Carrying heavy things that poke into you
- Smell of sweat and smoke and perfume and too strong deodorant
- Markers squeaking on the white board
- Buses braking...squeaking and hissing
- Engines humming...motors roaring
- Horns honking
- Doors slamming
- Talking...talking...more talking...louder talking
- Did it rain? Wet socks and shoes, more squeaky shoes
- Smelly soap in the bathrooms
- Hand dryers...way too loud
- Squeaking chairs and desks that are off balance
- Cold chairs in the summer with shorts
- Gym clothes
- People banging on tables

Looking Back:

There is a reason for why this list is important to me. If you went up to someone on the street and asked them about something they remember from school, I would guess that they would be likely to state a fact they learned or an important date they remember. This list contains all of the overwhelming sensory issues I had while I was in school. If you asked me what I remember most about school, I would not answer with facts of science or dates from history. I would answer with these memories of overstimulation.

<u>The Autism Community</u>

July 28, 2012 at 1:00 PM

I was going to try to paint how I felt about the autism community, but nothing seemed to be working out. My idea was going to be a painting of puzzle pieces divided by one thick jagged line with about a dozen words describing what divided the community. The biggest word was going to be "fear."

But the issue was that some of the words I picked out were also describing what brought the community together. "Parenting Techniques," for instance, was a phrase that describes what the community may disagree on, yet also find support in each other.

Basically, it was all too confusing. I thought, maybe I would just use the word "fear," but it just wasn't working out.

To be completely honest, my goal of the painting wasn't to say WHAT was dividing the autism community, but the fact that I don't think the community will ever UNITE. I don't think it can. It's similar to the idea of World Peace. We all WANT it, but we can't AGREE on how to GET it. There is always going to be someone who feels a different way, or feels the need to change someone's opinion, or just doesn't agree to disagree. Even though we all want to be united, I don't think we will. I don't want to be negative about it, but I just don't see it happening.

That brings me back to the word "fear." I fear what will happen to us, if we all continue to try to unite, and keep missing it. Will we have our own wars? Will we have our own groups? I fear that humanity will not be able to solve its issues, and instead of being united, we will be weak and divided amongst ourselves. I just wish we could all agree to disagree.

Things I'm Hypersensitive To

July 28, 2012 at 5:30 PM

I will do all of these in list form, so bear with me. These will be long, and I'll probably forget quite a few things.

Sounds

- ANYTHING that is louder than it usually is
- Sirens
- School bells
- Flagpoles clanging
- Alarm clocks
- Phones ringing
- The deep bass sound in music
- Doorbells
- Dishes clanging
- Bugs buzzing

- Vacuum cleaners
- Construction sounds
- Automobile engines, brakes squeaking, etc.
- Hair dryers (sometimes)
- Squeaky shoes/ similar squeaking
- Smoke detectors (one of the worst)
- High pitched sounds (dog barking, screams, lights/electronics, etc.)
- Anything that is not a consistent noise (changing in pitch, volume, or tempo, etc.)
- New sounds

Smells

- Perfume
- Deodorant
- Laundry detergent
- Soaps/shampoos/conditioners, etc.
- Cigarette smoke, cigar smoke (etc.)
- Hairspray
- Nail polish/ nail polish remover
- Body odors
- Vacuums (yes, they smell too!)
- Strong minty smells
- Spices
- Cleaning supplies
- Permanent markers
- Anything that YOU think smells bad

Sights

- Flickering things

- Lots of movement
- Quick things
- Brightness

Touch

- Tags on my clothing
- Things in my shoes
- Tickling
- Anything by my head
- Poking/tapping
- Wetness (wet clothing, hair, etc.)
- Loose hairs
- Stickiness
- Dry powders (chalk, dust, etc.)
- Tight (and I mean TIGHT) clothing
- Long sleeves/turtlenecks

I'm going to skip taste for now, because this is a strange one for me. (I'm a picky eater for different reasons.)

Looking Back:
There are a LOT of other things that I'm hypersensitive to. This is just a VERY short list to give people a basic idea of what kinds of things bother me.

Erin Clemens

Public Restrooms
July 29, 2012 at 5:15 PM

I've noticed a few times now, that parents have posted questions on various sites asking why their child will use the restroom at home, but not in public. While I can't specifically say that I know THE reason why, I can maybe give some insight into what COULD be causing some issues.

First, the hand driers. These hurt my ears to no extent. I literally have to plug my ears sometimes because the noise hurts so badly. My suggestion: bring ear plugs or head phones and music, and use Purell or bring your own paper towels.

Second, the fan. For me, personally, I NEED a fan. It keeps me calm, and the louder it is, the less likely someone else is to hear me or me to hear them. It gives me a sense of privacy. That being said, for other people it can be just as bad as the hand dryers.

Third, the smell. Bathrooms ALWAYS smell, but public bathrooms can be much worse. If it's THAT bad, I usually pull the neck of my shirt over my face. For others, it may be too intense. Or, you can try using face masks.

Fourth, differences in routine. Different toilet seat, different flushing sounds, different toilet paper, different soap and soap smells....you name it. Some places play music, some places have scented candles, some places have toilets that are higher or lower or colder. There isn't much I can do to suggest help with this one, other than keep the routine as similar as you can.

Please keep these ideas in mind, and understand that no one WANTS to go in their pants. It's just the lesser evil to the public restrooms for some people. Or, they don't know how to DEAL with the restroom, and end UP going in their pants. Or, it may be a different reason altogether. But these can hopefully give you SOME insights into what COULD be going on.

New Poem

July 30, 2012 at 11:25 AM

I usually don't know what to think, or what to say.
Sometimes, it just happens.
Like a light bulb is switched on.
But really, in the depths of my mind,
There is a huge machine.
It takes in little pieces of a broken picture,
And tries to piece them together,
In some way that seems to make sense.
Although they don't always quite fit.
Sometimes, the pictures don't come out right.
The pieces are left lying, scattered like shattered glass.
Left in the darkness, in the depths of my mind.
But the machine isn't broken.
It's just overworked.
It's taking a moment to build up power again.
And when it does,
The energy surges.
The lights come back on.
Pictures are formed again.

Fundraising At The Fair

August 5, 2012 at 10:05 AM

I've been SUPER busy all week. On Monday I went to the local fair. I found an autism booth, and (after buying a few items to help get iPads for kids) asked if I could join in! It was SO much fun. We met a lot of people who shared their stories with us, and educated many! The coolest part was the fact that the owner of the booth has a son on the opposite end of the spectrum from me. I love that when he and I were together, we could show just how different people with autism are from each other.

The fair itself was hard to tolerate sometimes. There was HORRIBLE technical feedback from the audio, lots of "winner" sirens going off all around us, people screaming, horsing around, and smoking. I ended up wearing my ear plugs half of the time.

In the end, though, we raised enough money for at least one iPad with an autism app, and we spread lots of awareness!

Doing The Right Thing

August 8, 2012 at 10:30 AM

I just love those times that can bring you to tears because someone did the right thing. I don't just mean following rules or laws. I mean going out of the way to do something that is right. I don't tend to see them as often as I'd like, but when I do, it just makes me SO happy. Here are some examples:

Someone returning a lost check to its address with information about where it was found, but not saying who THEY are. (You can't find them to thank them for the good deed.)

Someone picking up a piece of trash after a million people have walked by it.

Someone who stops by a homeless person lying in the middle of the room to make sure they are okay, and then giving them a bit of cash and telling them to move to a safer spot.

Someone who drives by a lemonade stand, but stops when they hear that it's for a fund raiser. They back up their car, give you extra money, and tell you to keep the change.

These are the kinds of moments that I absolutely love. It shows that there is still good in the world. It gives me hope.

And yes, these are all real-life examples.

Comfort Items

August 11, 2012 at 5:25 PM

Some people have a baby blanket they can't be without, or maybe a lucky charm, or a teddy bear. Usually, people will "outgrow" these things.

For me, I don't have a baby blanket or a lucky charm, and I don't "outgrow" my comfort items. Comfort items are what I use to keep myself calm and help myself to relax through-out the day. Without these items, I get so stressed and anxious that I cannot function. (My dog is not counted in this list because she is no longer alive and because I don't view her as an "item" but as a friend.)

My first item that I MUST have is my computer. My computer is what I go to when I'm mentally drained and NEED time to myself. It is my source to the outside world without having to function outside of my own comfort zone. It is my source of information, my connection to friends, my creative outlet, my personal memories, and my source of fun and relaxation. When my computer dies, I mentally and physically go into "emergency energy" mode, and use up all of the energy I have in the act of getting the computer fixed.

It's for this reason that when I got a blue screen on my computer the other day, I immediately turned it off and called the technicians. I brought it in, and they inspected it. When I got a message on my phone saying that I needed a new computer, I had a meltdown. In fact, I had 3 major meltdowns and at least 5 small meltdowns that day. I NEED my computer. I got a new one (just today) and I'm exhausted, but I'm getting better now.

The rest of my comfort items sort of come in random order. If I lose one, I try to fill the void with the others until I can get it fixed or replaced. But it HAS to be very similar to the one I already have.

My other comfort items:

My pillow and my bed (I can't sleep well otherwise).

My MP3 player (I have already used one of them until it died, and I bought the exact same one again and already used up the first battery).

My swing (took the place of my hammock which, after years of good use, fell out of the rotted wood that it was attached to).

My watch (can change in color, but MUST be the same brand and model).

My fiddle-stick (a toy I got at the Cracker Barrel store years ago).

My sound soother (my Mom got this for me, and it works WONDERS… I need only ONE of the sounds).

And I DO have one other comfort item that is kind of like a teddy bear, which is my Simba stuffed animal I've had since I was 7.

I have many other items in life that I like to remain the SAME all the time, but I could get USED to not having them or having them slightly changed.

Why?

August 12, 2012 at 10:00 AM

There are times when I find myself curious as to the reason behind things. Why does that person feel the way they do? Why did that person decide on what they did? Why does that person want me to do something?

I'm not asking these questions to be defiant, or to be digging in someone's business, or to make them feel bad, or to be rude, or anything like that. I'm asking these questions because they are truly genuine questions. I'm trying to understand the world around me.

There was one time, when I was younger and undiagnosed, that a neighbor asked me to put their dog outside. It was a hot day, and I was enjoying the dog's company myself, so I wanted to know why they wanted their dog outside. I simply asked them "Why?" They glared at me, and replied "Because I SAID to." I got really scared because I felt their anger. At that point, I didn't know why they wanted the dog outside OR why they were mad. In the end, I stopped asking, confused and scared, and put the dog outside. I went home feeling terrible and lost.

I don't blame this person for yelling at me. They didn't understand ME either. When I got home that day, I asked my mom the questions instead. Why did this person want the dog put outside, and why did they get mad at me when I asked for the reason? At this point in my life, I think my mom was starting to see that I misunderstood the world. She didn't know that I had Asperger's yet, but she was working to figure out what was going on. So she knew that my questions were genuine. She explained to me that asking "Why" when an adult asks you to do something can be seen as defiant or rude. She told me that it was a miscommunication. She also told me that it wasn't my dog, so I need to listen to owners' requests. I understood all of this. But I still wish people wouldn't assume the worst with me.

The Newspaper

August 14, 2012 at 10:00 AM

I want to take a moment to thank the newspaper staff for doing a project on the autistic spectrum, and giving me the opportunity to lead it.

I Have Asperger's

Since before I was diagnosed, and still sometimes after, I've struggled to be heard. People sometimes think that my opinion is useless. How could I possibly understand autism if I can actually TALK to them? Well, at least that's what it seems like people are asking me when they say "but you don't SEEM like you have Asperger's."

But I do. And I could really give an insight to what it's like, at least for me. The awkward misunderstandings, the overwhelming hypersensitivities, the calming feeling of self-stimming, the awesome talents that seem to come naturally, and the beauty of being different.

The newspaper gave me a chance to share this with my community, along with some others who wanted to have a voice. They gave me a chance to show people a raw look at what it's really like on the spectrum, not just for one person, but for a few different people on different parts on the spectrum.

It means a lot to me to know that people out there are willing to listen and share not just my story, but a few different stories from the autism community.

So thank you, to the wonderful, kind staff.

A Voice

August 14, 2012 at 11:45 AM

I know I'm really fortunate to be able to speak out loud, because there are many on the spectrum who have a hard time speaking in words. However, I DO have a hard time communicating. Just because I can form words, doesn't mean that I can efficiently communicate with others.

Many times, people tend to misunderstand what I'm trying to say, or the other way around. People seem to assume I know or understand something, and this can cause more problems. Sometimes, people even get mad because they think I said one thing, but I really mcant something else. I can speak out loud, but it's very difficult to make sense of things.

It must be very frustrating to not be able to form words and speak to others. I do realize that. Speaking out loud is not the only part of communication, though. And it's really hard when people seem to expect that simply because I can speak, the Asperger's doesn't interfere with communication. But in fact, it's VERY hard for me to process the conversation, and most of the time I'm guessing or don't even realize that I don't get it.

So next time you ask someone "are they verbal?" know that it's only one piece of the equation.

Surprises

August 14, 2012 at 2:05 PM

I've seen videos on TV or YouTube where people are scared or surprised, and then they end up laughing about it. You know the ones. They have a creepy picture pop up on a computer screen, or they are tricked into thinking they won the lottery. I hate these videos, because I can't understand why people enjoy that feeling.

To me, being scared or tricked HURTS. It's like being shocked with a bolt of electricity. It can send me into a panic attack. I will never forget one day, near Halloween, I was at the mall and I saw a costume. I walked over to it to look at it more closely, and it turned out to be a person. Yes, the person jumped at me. After screaming I started to cry. Now, don't get me wrong. I can set MYSELF up to be scared a little. But it's usually under my own control, such as a DVD or an amusement park ride that I have already been on. (With new rides, I HAVE to look at videos of them first so that I know what to expect, otherwise I don't usually go on the new ones.) But knowing that someone is going to surprise me can be just as bad as being scared.

When someone tells me that they have a surprise for me, I need to know right then and there what the surprise is. Otherwise, I get really anxious and stressed out. Is it a BIG surprise? I don't want to be let down, but I can't imagine the little surprises. (I tend to dream big sometimes.) If you have a surprise for me and you CAN'T tell me what it is, you AT LEAST have to tell me EXACTLY when to expect it. Otherwise, don't tell me that you have a surprise for me until you give it to me, because even if I know when to expect it, I'm still going to be anxious and stressed up until that ment. Again, if you are going to surprise me, be gentle when you surprise me, and don't say a word to me about it until the minute you give it to me.

I Am ME

August 20, 2012 at 9:30 PM

I've noticed that the autism community seems to be struggling to stay united. I've also noticed that it's often because people have very different points of view.

That's because people ARE different.

I don't like when someone starts using words like *everyone*, *all*, *none*, *always*, *never*, or any kind of "percent." (Believe me, I'm guilty of doing this as well!)

I am not Rain Man, I am not Temple Grandin (though, she is one of my heroes!), I am ME. I am only ONE of the MANY different people who are on the autism spectrum. We are DIFFERENT. Not just from the neurotypical people, but from each other as well.

I try to remember to use expressions such as *in my opinion*, *I think*, *for me*, etc. Of course, I will occasionally forget and start talking as though I am speaking for EVERYONE. (I make mistakes, too!) I am still learning that I am NOT the only one out there with Asperger's, and that my viewpoints are just that: My OWN.

That's not to say that there haven't been people who agree with me. In fact, I know a LOT of people who go "YES! That's ME!" However, I've encountered many who also say "You know, I don't quite feel the same way." And I'd like to respect that.

So, please, the next time you describe me, make sure that you get to know who I am first, because I am an individual.

<u>School</u>

August 24, 2012 at 9:15 PM

I was diagnosed with Asperger's when I was in 10th grade, at about 15 years old. I wish I had been diagnosed earlier so that my parents would have been able to get me out of mainstream school quicker. But my parents fought hard and at least I was out of mainstreaming for the last two years of my school career.

I know that I'm not the same as everyone else on the spectrum, but it's because of my experience of the difficulty in getting OUT of mainstream school, that I CRINGE when parents of children on the spectrum say that they are going to TRY it. I can only remember my personal experiences and how difficult they were. The daily panic attacks, the misunderstanding from teachers and students alike, everything.

So while I know that this is only MY opinion, I personally feel that some people on the spectrum would be better off home-schooled. At least until schools are better equipped, educated and have a better budget to actually give the student on the spectrum a quality education. (I won't get into this part because I hate politics.)

How I Got Through School

August 26, 2012 at 9:15 AM

First, let me say that it wasn't easy. In fact, it was THE hardest time in my entire life. I was undiagnosed and misunderstood. I also misunderstood others. Teachers would always say that I was doing fine, but I WASN'T. I was only coping.

My first way of coping was by doing as much as I could to remain in control. I watched the clock and the seconds ticking on my personal watch. I learned EXACTLY when the bell would ring. This helped me to prepare myself for the bell, as well as give me the maximum amount of time I could have to get to my next class. I needed all of the time I could get, for many reasons. One was the idea that it took me time to process what people were saying, what was going on, what I needed to do, etc. The more time I could give myself, the better off I was. This especially came into play for the use of my next coping skill: the bathroom.

Now, part of the development in the bathroom coping skill was because I became SO fearful that my bladder was instinctively telling me I had to go. It's like when someone has a nightmare and wets the bed. But I soon realized that going to the bathroom between classes gave me one of the biggest breaks in school. I could go into a stall and be alone for literally about 30 seconds. (Which, at that point, was amazing. That's how bad things were...usually I need about 15 minutes to break, but I took whatever time I could get.)

Another coping skill I used was sitting as close to the door of the classroom as I possibly could. This enabled me to be closer to the teacher (so I felt more protected....most of the time), closer to the exit so I wouldn't feel so trapped, and it enabled me to be the first one out of the classroom at the end, somewhat avoiding the quick chaos that filled the hallways in the few seconds after the bell rang.

The next coping skill I can think of was to bring with me as much of the supplies I needed through-out the day as possible. This eliminated MANY locker trips, keeping me away from the chaos of the locker bays and saving me more time. (There's that time word again!) I also felt the comfort in having all of the items with me and close to me, in case I ever needed something for comfort or just for the class. I also started to realize that if there was ever a fire drill (or a real fire) I needed to have something small I could carry with me so that I didn't lose the important items. This made me feel safer, too. I had plans.

In the end, I would find ways to stay alive. Literally. If it weren't for these plans and skills I developed, I wouldn't have been able to survive school. I almost didn't even WITH them.

Sometimes, the sign that a student is not doing well is when they look like they are doing well ACADEMICALLY, but THEY say they are not "doing well." Maybe, just MAYBE, the student is NOT referring to their academics, but to their health.

Concerns

August 28, 2012 at 2:55 PM

I'm beginning to notice a possible mental health issue that we may be facing. In life, many kids on the spectrum will turn into adults and will leave their parents and live on their own. At this point, many of the parents go through that infamous "empty nest syndrome." They are sad that their children are gone and don't have them at home to take care of anymore. This is understandable for a parent to experience. Not only do they probably have an instinct to continue to protect their "child," but after many years of living with them, parents are now alone. The same issue is for the child. They have lived with their parents telling them what to do, when, and how. Once the child has moved out, they can finally begin to learn how to figure out these answers on their own. THIS is what I feel it means to become an independent adult. Sure, every once in a while, the child can call the parents and ask for some help, but for the most part, they can navigate through life.

The issue is when the economy is bad, and the child can no longer afford to live on their own. What choice do they have other than to move back in with their parents? At a time in a person's life when it is essential for them to learn how to survive without the parents' help, they are forced into depending on them once more. And the parents are once again finding themselves with their children to care for. Even though they really don't have to actually "parent" them, it's their instinct to do so. THEN, when the child can leave again, the parents may go through that "empty nest syndrome" a second time.

I know I will be on the lookout for the repercussions of this issue.

I Have A Dream

August 29, 2012 at 9:25 AM

In honor of and inspired by Dr. Martin Luther King, Jr.

I have a dream.

I have a dream that one day, children and adults of all ages will be heard when they feel no one is listening. I have a dream that everyone will have an education that suits the way each and every individual learns best. I have a dream that no one will be judged by their "disabilities," but by their abilities. I have a dream that one day everyone will find that their differences will be appreciated. I have a dream that no parent will ever feel guilty for something of which they are not at fault. I have a dream that positivity will overpower negativity when people come together for a cause. I have a dream that stereotypes will one day no longer exist, and each person will be seen as the individual they are.

And I have a dream, that one day, these dreams I have may come true.

Asking For Help

September 1, 2012 at 11:20 AM

For some reason, it's very difficult for me to ask for help. It can be hard to find exactly what I need help WITH, and THEN I have to communicate it the right way so that people understand.

For example: No, I don't need you to PHYSICALLY help me clean my room, I need you to help me MENTALLY from being overwhelmed, and keep me on task. A great school example: I understand that I have to do 10 minutes of reading tonight for homework, but WHAT do I have to read? (Only to find out the next day that I have to ALSO REMEMBER what I'm reading because there's an assignment based on the material.)

That's part one. Part two is when I know I STILL don't understand what you have just tried to help me with, and I don't know how to let you know that I appreciate you trying to help, but it WASN'T helpful. I still need MORE help. This part leads me to feel bad, and I end up just not getting the help I need because I don't want to keep bothering people.

So NOW, I don't even like to ask people for help until the LAST second, when it may be too late, and then people get mad that I've waited so long. (I've been working on this issue for years.) Sometimes, I also feel so frozen because I'm lacking the self-confidence to do something on my own, and I wait for the help. Then people think I'm being lazy because I am asking for help with doing something I could probably do on my own instead of developing skills I don't have yet.

Sometimes, my brain is screaming "help me!" and my mouth just can't form the words because of all of these thoughts.

Irony

September 4, 2012 at 3:25 PM

Sometimes, you just have to laugh at bad days. Today was the first day of school for the local district. Last night, I had 2 terrible nightmares. I could hardly think when I was at work due to the continuous flashbacks I was having. (I have flashbacks because I have Post Traumatic Stress Disorder from my school experiences.) They were so awful and by the time I got back home I was a mess. I just had one after another, and I was at the point where I was just rocking myself sobbing. Finally, I called my Mom, who reminded me to take a medication (which helped!) and told me to come home when I was able to drive. I talked to my therapist, which also helped a bit. Then I went to see my Mom. Most of the flashbacks have pretty much subsided, so I was able to do some laundry and be with my Mom. I even got to visit a neighbor. I was feeling pretty well when I left, and THEN I started seeing the school buses again. One after another, I could barely stand it. I thought to myself "Just get home."

So where's the irony in my story? When I turned into the parking lot of the apartments I live in, WAITING for me there, was a school bus. RIGHT outside MY apartment. Literally, right outside MY door. After cursing every word I could think of, I just had to laugh.

And at the very moment I type this, I'm hearing it start up and leave.

Asperger's As An Excuse

September 10, 2012 at 11:00 AM

I hate "using" my Asperger's diagnosis as an "excuse." I don't want people to think I'm trying to get the easy way out, or not taking responsibility for my actions. I try not to take more help than I need, or ask for unnecessary accommodations. I will apologize for my wrong doings, and try everything in the world to make it right. However, I'm starting to notice that there are times when people are unfairly mad at me for things that I struggle with. It could be misunderstanding someone, forgetting social etiquette, reacting to hypersensitivities, or just being unaware of what's going on or how to deal with something. First, I will have to try and explain that I'm struggling with something, and the person must know already that I have Asperger's. If not, I will politely tell them that I do. When people are unfairly mad at me for these things, however, I feel it is fair for me to "play the Asperger's card." This means REMINDING them that I have Asperger's, and that I will always work on these weaknesses that I have, but for them to be upset with me for being unable to explain my actions to them other than that I have Asperger's, they need to cut me SOME slack. I hardly EVER "use" my Asperger's as an "excuse," so when I do, I hope people realize that it's seriously a struggle for me to explain something.

Looking Back:

After sharing this post on Twitter one day, someone replied explaining to me that the situations I described are not using Asperger's as an "excuse," but as a REASON.

Autism Speaks Walk
September 15, 2012 at 3:10 PM

I had the most amazing time today. The people from Autism Speaks gave me a free booth at which I could share my website information and sell my Autism Awareness Duct Tape Bracelets. I made AT LEAST $250 that will go to charity. I also got to share my newspaper articles. This wasn't all I was given, though.

I actually had the amazing opportunity to speak on stage, in front of almost 15,000 people. My hope is that even if only ONE person hears me, they will be inspired. They won't give up. After I spoke, I took a picture of the crowd as they started out on their 1 mile walk. It was very moving. (The crowd literally was!)

This is what I said when I was on stage:

10 years ago, I struggled with school. People had a hard time understanding my behavior, and I couldn't articulate my feelings because of my autism. Today, I am a successful advocate, blogger, public speaker, and artist. I live independently, I drive, and I have friends from all over the world because I tell the stories of those with autism in a way that people can understand. My hope is that in another 10 years, I will be joined by many of you out there in the audience. Together, we can create a future where autism is openly talked about, respected, and accepted.

The Goal

September 16, 2012 at 9:25 PM

There are SO MANY different organizations, groups, websites, and more that want to share their opinions about autism. I have seen people who are political, people who are for a cure, people who are against a cure, and people who really don't know WHAT to think. But we need ALL of these people, because we all have a story. What I'm learning is that, even if I don't agree with how someone treats MY opinions, that doesn't mean that the person isn't doing good work. If you disagree with someone's point of view, distance yourself from them, and focus on your own view. Focus on getting YOUR story told. Because, isn't that our goal in the end? For everyone to be able to tell their story? We don't HAVE to stand TOGETHER. We just have to stand.

What Is High Functioning?

September 20, 2012 at 9:50 AM

This blog post in NO WAY is intended to offend anyone. If I have said something that is offensive, please accept my apologies. This is my point of view only.

Sometimes, people on the autism spectrum are referred to as "low functioning" or "high functioning." I've been asked many times by others "what does 'high functioning' mean?" Great question! I don't think anyone really knows the definition to this one, because it's sort of like asking, "what is normal?" At the same time, why do the different levels of the spectrum seem so obvious to some people? Are the levels actually different? Maybe they're not fully understood.

If I had to define “high functioning,” my best way of describing it would be (and I still feel that this definition needs more to it):

A person on the spectrum who can better find ways to cope with the world around them.

Now, this DOES NOT mean that the person is any less AFFECTED by the world. Everything is just as difficult, but instead of having a meltdown because a sound is too loud, they have learned to cover their ears, use ear plugs, headphones, or some other way of COPING with the issue. What seems to be even more difficult is that the person is not as noticeably in distress. So now, they are not only in distress, but people around them don't even know it.

I'm not at all trying to say that someone who is "high functioning" is any worse off than someone who is "low functioning." I am merely trying to express what I feel is the difference that people are seeing which has led to the different levels. Everyone on the spectrum has their own struggles, and everyone has their own achievements.

School Textbooks

September 20, 2012 at 8:35 PM

I read part of a textbook that a 6th grade girl brought home, and one of the questions in the book said "Reading Check! Where do most of Colombia's people live?" So, just to see if I could answer the question, I read over the page. Someone on the autism spectrum may not have been able to answer this question. Rather than specifically saying somewhere "Most of Colombia's people live in...." it said "Nearly 80 percent of Colombia's people live in...". This is not a "reading" check, this is a COMPREHENSION check. This is the type of thing I struggled with in school.

Continuing on, I figured I would see if there was anything else on that page that would confuse me. The confusion was never-ending! Under "Applying Map Skills" was the question, "What bodies of water does Colombia border?" Well, there were rivers going all through it. LOTS of them. In 6th grade, I would have counted these as bodies of water, because Colombia "land" technically "bordered" this water. I would have listed each river and stream I saw labeled. THEN, I would have listed the oceans and seas. The NEXT question in that section was easy, IF I'd heard the question out loud: "What country has a name that sounds like *Equator*?" Hopefully I read that word correctly; otherwise, I'm never going to find the answer!

This is what I would have struggled with already, and I hadn't even turned the PAGE.

Acceptance

September 30, 2012 at 7:40 AM

I know I posted something very similar to this before, but I feel like I should post it again. There are so many people in the autism community. Not everyone in the community believes in the same things. Some people want a cure, some people want research, some people want services, some people want more funding, and some people JUST want their story to be heard. I feel as though we are all COMPETING, and I truly feel that the competition is driving the community apart. The truth is, however, we don't HAVE to agree on everything. We don't HAVE to agree on whether we need a cure, more or less research, services, or funding. To ask everyone in the community to stand for ALL of these ideas is like asking for world peace. It's not going to happen. However, there is ONE thing I feel that the entire community can agree on, and that is for acceptance. In fact, who WOULDN'T want to be accepted? So, whether we unite over this ONE idea or we have to each stand alone for it, we can all at least try to stand. Stand for acceptance. Not just for people with autism, but for everyone. We may not ever be able to completely unite, but we can try to get a little bit closer.

Time

October 5, 2012 at 10:35 AM

Time is such an amazing thing. It heals people. It teaches people countless lessons. It allows us to grow. Some people need more time than others, and some people need more time than they may have. There have been moments where I feel like time will do nothing to help, but it seems to pull me through. When you feel that nothing else can help you through, give yourself time and see what happens.

Happy Birthday

October 5, 2012 at 11:15 AM

To my best friend, forever and always.

You were there for me through thick and thin. When I needed you the most, you were there. You taught me how to grow and become the person who I want to be. Through your unconditional love, you taught me how to forgive. You kept me healthy, reminding me to go for walks. You kept me on time, waking me up in the mornings. You kept me light hearted and happy. You kept me alive and going when I didn't think I could go on. You gave me strength to conquer my fears. You inspired me to create artwork. You reminded me to enjoy the little things in life. And even when you are gone, you continue to teach me, for now you are teaching me how to let go.

Happy Birthday, my beloved friend. May you always rest in peace.

For my dog.

Born October 5th, 1999

Died June 5th, 2012

Temple Grandin
October 9, 2012 at 7:40 AM

The other day, I had the most AMAZING opportunity. I had the chance to speak with the one and only Temple Grandin over the phone. I was able to tell her that she is one of my heroes. She gave me lots of advice on how to move further in my animal career. I learned that Omega 3 oils may HELP with the hypersensitivities, even though it may take a couple months to start working, and it's not a "cure." Another thing I learned (that I probably knew, and just wouldn't listen to anyone else!) was that I need to eat better and get more exercise. Did you know that she does 100 sit-ups a day? Yeah, that impressed me, too!

She is a really down-to-earth person, in my opinion. Someone who really loves to work hard and live healthy. I thank her for taking time out of her day to talk with me and give me advice.

Sprained Foot

October 23, 2012 at 8:50 AM

I sprained my foot a few weeks ago. NOT my ankle. My FOOT. (People always get confused about this.) How did I sprain it? Well, I will tell you the EXCITING (yet untrue) story that the banker told me to share first:

"I was trying to save a burning bus from falling off of a HUGE cliff. As I was pulling it back, saving the lives of MANY people, it rolled over my foot. Miraculously, I only sprained my foot and sustained no other injuries!"

Okay, okay. The truth? When I was dancing, I stepped on the little metal piece that connects carpet flooring to tile flooring. I landed on it in JUST the right spot that I happened to sprain the bottom of my foot.

See why I go with the banker's story? ☺

It's just my luck that it also happens to be my driving foot. So I can't drive right now, either. I was able to get a ride to the doctor though, and I am on crutches. I have to ice my foot for 20 minutes, 5 times a day. This has led me to another interesting situation: routine.

I ice my foot at 9am, 12pm, 3pm, 6pm and 9pm. This is my strict schedule. It keeps me on time and if it changes at all, I get messed up. My foot is wrapped up when I ice it because otherwise it's WAY too cold. This schedule usually works because I tend to wake up between 8 and 8:30am. It gives me time to let my morning medicine (for focus) get into my system while I get dressed and wrap my foot. Then I ice it at 9am. Well, one morning, I happened to wake up at 8:50am. What a meltdown I had! I was too groggy and unfocused to realize that I don't HAVE to ice my foot 5 times. It's okay to miss it ONCE. I scrambled to get myself dressed, but my medicine wasn't going to be in my system in time, and so trying to wrap my foot in a bandage was like trying to tie shoes when your hands are numb. I ended up in a meltdown until my medicine was in and I realized that I was okay.

Now I understand that I could even ice my foot 10 minutes early or late if I need to. But when I was half-asleep and my medicine wasn't in, that black and white concept of "do or don't" was all I could see.

I go back to the doctor on Friday. Hopefully, my foot will be healed soon!

Update

November 9, 2012 at 8:30 PM

I know it's been a while since I've written. First off, my apparent "foot sprain" is officially a minor "stress fracture" of my heel. The good news is that I can start driving again soon, and I only have to wear the boot the doctor gave me for 2 more weeks.

Now, one of the main reasons I haven't written is because I get a lot of comments on my website, but I don't always know what they mean, the tone behind them, or how to respond. It kind of throws me off and I don't know what to do next. So while I LOVE to see the comments, I don't know HOW to reply to them. I don't want people to think that I'm ignoring them; I just honestly don't know what to do in response.

I have a big fundraiser event I was invited to tomorrow, so I need to get ready for that now. Hopefully my dress will match my medical boot! (I've already decorated it with some blue!)

I'm NOT "Normal"

November 16, 2012 at 7:20 PM

I want people to know things about me. When you first meet me, you wouldn't know that I'm an Aspie. In fact, you probably wouldn't even notice that anything about me is different. But that's where my biggest issue is. No, I don't use an iPad to communicate. I CAN drive. I CAN work. I DO live independently. This is what throws people off. Everyone seems to have this crazy idea that people with ASD are incapable of doing these things. It's not that they are incapable. It's that they are not ready. And they may never be ready. I just happened to be ready sooner. So yes, I am VERY verbal, but my communication skills are not easy. I have a hard time interpreting what people say, and figuring out how to respond. I can barely work a part time job for an hour or two before I feel like I've taken the SAT tests. I can only drive on certain roads to a certain distance. I live independently, but I need people to help me daily in my apartment. I may not be your obvious person with

ASD, but that's what makes MY life challenging. I don't want to have to prove that I have Asperger's. I have worked so hard to make it in this world. I haven't always been this way, either. I nearly dropped out and wanted to die in 10th grade. But the point is that I'm still here. I know that others are still struggling, but I also know that I have had my share of struggles too. And so please, don't EVER call me "normal." I take that as a complete insult.

Thanksgiving

November 22, 2012 at 5:40 PM

First off, I hope that everyone in the U.S. has had a happy Thanksgiving.

Second, I want to say that although I'm thankful for many things (Dad cooking an AMAZING dinner, friends, family, health, etc.), I am NOT thankful for Thanksgiving itself.

There are SO MANY: Noises, people, smells, types of food, hustling, shouting, laughing, dishes clanging, and stores closed - the list goes on and on. And there's NO mail. (Any day that takes mail away from me is automatically starting off on the "downhill" end.)

But not only do these situations bother me, they last ALL DAY. There's no way to escape from the madness. And family would think you are being rude if you stay away. In reality, I would LOVE to be able to join people, but I just don't enjoy the time.

So I am thankful that Thanksgiving only lasts one day...how's that?

Black Friday

November 23, 2012 at 7:45 PM

People always tell me that I'm crazy for enjoying Black Friday. But besides getting up early (and maybe being a little cold), they should come with me and see what I experience. I don't go to the stupid stores like Walmart (cheapest department store) or Best Buy (cheapest electronics store) or even the mall. I go to ONE shopping center close to home. Every year I've gone (at least three in a row now) there have been no more than 15 people total waiting in a line outside a store. LAST year, Staples (an electronics store) gave out free coffee and doughnuts! THIS year, no one even WAITED in line for another electronics store, and I was the first (and only) one in when they opened. When I go, I plan ahead. I know what I want, how much I will spend, and what time the store will open. I have had HUGE success in the past 3 years that I have gone. I don't think there was one year that I didn't get what I planned to. And every year I save a LOT. So, while I understand the REGULAR madness is ridiculous (terrible driving, pushing and shoving, waiting in line 24 hours ahead, going at midnight, etc.), the way I personally do Black Friday is actually a really nice experience where I've met some nice people and had a good time.

Winter & Spring, 2012-2013

Art

December 1, 2012 at 8:45 AM

I've been a little depressed lately, so I decided to try and do some art to let out the emotions. The first piece I did was probably the most personal. I call it "Meltdown," and it's supposed to represent the results of meltdowns that I've had through-out my life.

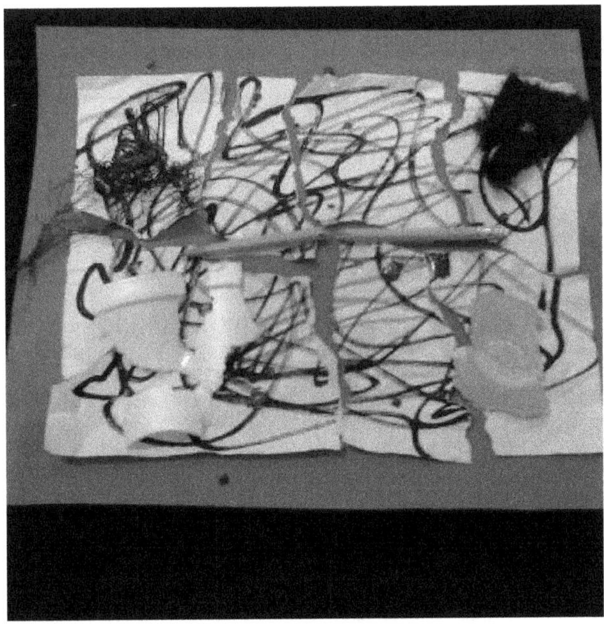

I Have Asperger's

There are scribbles, a crumpled up and ripped piece of paper, string (to represent hair), a torn piece of cloth, and broken items among other things.

I know that it looks like a huge mess, as though a toddler could put this together, but when you look closely you will see that it's really precise in the way it's been made. It represents that although I may seem to act like a child during my meltdowns, it's actually something that I still do today as an adult. I've also learned through the years how to better handle my meltdowns so that these sort of things do not happen as a result....sometimes. Another thought I'd like to add is how this may seem to represent a tantrum, but it is NOT a tantrum. Meltdowns are different from tantrums.

My Hamster Has Autism

December 5, 2012 at 6:35 PM

Some people think I'm kidding when I say that my hamster has autism, but I'm not kidding. I actually think he could have autism. Here are the traits that make me believe this:

1. He doesn't like to be touched. I'm not talking about the idea that he may not like to be held for very long. I'm talking about the idea that he only tolerates me touching him if he is distracted because I'm going to give him food. He HATES to be held. Yet, if I hold him tight enough, he doesn't squirm. But if I just gently pick him up, he resists with all of his might.

2. He doesn't like change. Instead of being excited to explore new objects, he ignores them and pushes them away (unless it's a food he likes the smell of). He doesn't like new chew toys, though. In

fact, he is VERY strict with his routine. (I may influence this part, however.)

3. He does NOT like to be outside of a familiar environment. (Sort of goes with change...) He has resisted his hamster ball so many times that I feel bad I ever made him try it out. He hated the cardboard box maze that I tried to make for him. Instead, he is much happier with the wheel inside his cage. Which brings me to...

4. He hyper-focuses on his wheel. It's as though it's a safe haven for him. And when I've finished cleaning his cage and I put him back in, he doesn't hesitate to go right into his wheel for some quiet time. That's the interesting part. He doesn't just run in his wheel, he SITS in it. Or he will take one or two steps and peek his head out. (It's an enclosed wheel that is a part of the cage design). It's almost as though it's a self stim for him. And when he isn't running or walking in it, sometimes he even SLEEPS in it. And if a piece of food gets stuck in it from EATING in the wheel, he tries to move it out of the way so it won't make so much noise.

Now, some of these traits may be common for hamsters, but to have all of these traits together is just very interesting to me. I like to think that he is like me, and might be a little bit on the autism spectrum.

I Did It!

December 12, 2012 at 8:40 AM

I finally did something I've been wanting and waiting to do ALL YEAR! But wait, I'm getting ahead of myself.

I Have Asperger's

One of the things I like to do as part of autism advocacy is make and sell Autism Awareness Duct Tape Bracelets, and then donate that money to help others with autism. I started doing it a few years ago in April. I was only going to do it for Autism Awareness Month, but then I realized how well they sold. This year, I made them all year long. I sold them at presentations, at a local fair, at an Autism Speaks walk, and more. I was aiming to make more than what I had made last year, which was about $200. Well, I beat that number alright! I sold so many bracelets that I ended up with over $800! This time, I couldn't JUST donate the money. I wanted to do something more.

So, I went out and bought an iPad AND a military grade case and screen protector. I'm going to donate it to a class that has 7 kids on the autism spectrum. One of the parents had requested an iPad for the classroom, and the school said that they didn't have the money for it. Well, now they will get one! I hope to be there to present it to them. Oh, did I mention that I ended up with more than $100 left over? I hope they can use that money towards an app or two.

Asperger's Diagnosis

December 14, 2012 at 7:20 PM

This is something I wrote in response to the removal of Asperger's Syndrome from the DSM.

I will never forget a quote from the television show *House M.D.* when House says, "When we are born, we are perfect. 10 fingers, 10 toes, pink and plump. It all goes downhill from there." The sad thing is, what he said was true in the eyes of most parents. They think that this description is considered a "perfect baby". But it's not. It's just a common form.

I was born how most people see is the "perfect baby." I had 10 fingers and 10 toes. I was pink and plump. But hidden within my brain was something different from some other babies. I was born with Asperger's Syndrome, a form of autism. Then again, you might also be able to say that I was born like MANY other babies on the spectrum. ☺

I guess what I'm trying to say is that yes, I am different from some. I LIKE being different. I like that I finally know the name of what makes me different. People finally understand me because I say to them, "I have Asperger's." I'm not saying to them that I have autism, unless I'm referring to being on the autism spectrum. (Not that I think autism is "bad," just that I'm not ACTUALLY diagnosed with autism itself.) I am SO PROUD to call myself an "Aspie." I've found a huge part of my identity.

Then, in December of 2012, I learned something tragic. I will no longer be considered an "Aspie" in 2013. NO ONE will be considered an "Aspie." That's because the diagnosis of "Asperger's Syndrome" will be dropped from the DSM. Think about it as if someone told you that you are one gender, and then YEARS later, they say, "Oh, that gender will not exist anymore. Instead, you will just be a part of this gender."

How am I no longer this person I've been for so many years? How have I CHANGED? I HAVEN'T. People will see me differently JUST BECAUSE a word is dropped. Will people treat me differently? Maybe. Should I be treated differently? Maybe. Maybe I want to be treated with more respect, and perhaps I WILL be treated with more respect. But it won't be because I changed, it will be because people THINK I changed. They automatically see me as someone different.

People hardly believe me when I tell them I have Asperger's. I already have to somehow "prove" to them that I have it. (Ridiculous, I know.) Soon, I will have to tell them that I have "high-functioning autism." No one will believe THAT. I will no longer be able to say that I have a "form of autism." I will no longer be able to say that I'm an "Aspie." Autism means a lot to me, but I still have Asperger's Syndrome. Whether it's in the book or not, I refuse to let them take away a piece of my identity that helped others to understand me more. My Twitter name is @AspergerSadie. My website is www.ihaveaspergers.webs.com .

And all of this is only ME. This doesn't include countless others who may even LOSE their diagnosis. Friends of mine. Why do other people get to decide who is in the autism community? Instead of trying to change our titles, LISTEN to what WE have to say.

Keeping Traditions

December 16, 2012 at 10:10 PM

I think my family is finally starting to understand the intense feeling I have for things needing to stay the same. With traditions in our family, I remember them down to a 'T.' My family is finally starting to realize how much I love it and how respected I feel when they ask me exactly how we do things because they forget these details. Things like: Whose stocking goes on which hook above the fireplace? Which Christmas CD do we listen to during which tradition? What order do we open gifts? I know these details. And they are important to me because they give me a sense of stability and comfort. They help me to stay prepared and let me better deal with things.

In Memory of 12/14/12

December 17, 2012 at 4:30 PM

I feel hurt about the tragedy in Connecticut. So this is what I want to write:

I am not a mother. I cannot begin to understand the devastation that all parents must be going through. I may never know the terror that those children felt. I would love to understand these feelings and be able to express empathy, but I cannot. However, it is not because I do not care.

I care about each and every one of the 20 children who were lost. I care about the teachers and staff who died bravely saving many other children. I am sorry to the shooter's family for the loss of the mother and for the sad actions that the shooter felt he had to take. I am sorry to my friends in the autism community who have been unfairly declared by media as "violent." I wish the arguments about gun violence and religion in schools would go away. I wish that people could feel hope and love again. I wish that for once, I could really truly know each victim, who they were, and remember them for how they lived.

Not how they died.

A Message To Autism Advocates

December 21, 2012 at 1:10 PM

I want to take a moment to step back and be proud. While we had a tragedy, we also had a unity.

The events in Connecticut have brought out a lot of confusion and misunderstanding about Asperger's and the Autistic Spectrum. I don't even know HOW it began, but someone reports that a suspect MIGHT be on the Autistic Spectrum, and everything goes helter-skelter. All of the sudden, all of these people believe that autism makes people monstrous planners of mass murders. But WE KNOW THIS IS NOT TRUE.

And while I was terrified for the autism community and the connections made, I was so relieved to see so many people writing in defense. SO many advocates who I didn't hear from as often stepped up to the plate to debunk the myths. So many people with the courage to stand up to a world where they aren't easily accepted (for some strange reason...but that's another blog post for another day...).

I'm proud because I saw, just for a glimpse, the Autistic community UNITE. We all knew that we had to do our part in teaching the world and that we had to do it QUICKLY.

So thank you to all of my friends and to the strangers as well for speaking out about the fact that people on the autism spectrum are different, and that our ASD is NOT linked to planned violence.

Happy New Year!
January 2, 2013 at 8:35 AM

Okay, 2012 was certainly an interesting year. Thankfully, it was mostly a good one for me. Here are just a few of the awesome things that happened:

- My dog was able to sing "Happy Birthday" to me one more time
- I moved out of my parents' house
- I did SEVERAL big autism presentations
- I was on TV twice talking about autism
- I led a project about autism (making the front page) in my local newspaper
- I spoke at the Walk Now for Autism Speaks in front of nearly 15,000 people
- I made and sold enough Autism Awareness Duct Tape Bracelets to be able to buy an iPad and case for others
- I got my hamster, Charlie
- I spoke to Temple Grandin.

The main negative things that happened this year (I'm limiting this list because I want to stay happy) would be:

- My dog passed away
- Hurricane Sandy
- The tragedy in Connecticut.

So to be honest, I'm MOSTLY happy with 2012. I can only hope that 2013 brings me at least the same amount of happiness. But I know that I don't do well looking really far ahead, so I'm going to take this year one day at a time. And yesterday didn't count because it was a holiday. I start my 2013 on January 2nd! (Unless of course this day goes badly...then we start over again.)

Define Me

January 5, 2013 at 8:25 PM

I know that many people may disagree, but I actually don't mind being defined by my Asperger's. I enjoy it. I see it as a strength and something that makes me unique and amazing. What I mind is when people start negatively associating my Asperger's with my limitations, and then defining me by THEM. That's unfair, because we ALL have limitations. We also all have strengths, and without my Asperger's, my strengths would be very different.

Define me by my Asperger's, if you want to. Define me by my artistic skills, my different way of seeing things, and my other unique talents. I am not ashamed to have Asperger's.

My Problems With Earplugs

January 8, 2013 at 9:50 AM

Earplugs can really come in handy when you are at a rock concert or when you have a baby and it's your turn to sleep. They can also come in handy when you are on the autism spectrum. They can help make it so that hand dryers in bathrooms don't hurt my ears, or when I'm in a crowd and I'm overwhelmed and overstimulated.

The problem is...well, actually I have a few problems with them. In fact, I hardly ever use them unless I'm at a rock concert or in a crowd at some other sort of event. These are most of the issues I have with them:

They can be annoying to put in. It takes a good amount of time just trying to adjust them to feel right and fit well.

They block out only PART of the loud noises, and they block out a LOT of the quieter ones. (This is obvious, but I like some of the quieter ones.)

People either think you are rude for wearing them (or think you are ignoring them), or look at you like you are crazy.

Again, they block out some of the quieter noises that I WANT to hear. Noises like someone walking towards me, my phone vibrating (I don't always feel the vibration, but I tend to hear it), and any other noises that help me to prepare myself for what may be about to happen. (I'll see if I can explain this in another post sometime.)

All in all, I hardly ever wear ear plugs. More often than not, I find myself using my hands to just cover my ears for a moment or two until the worst sounds have passed. Yet I also know many others on the spectrum who find them to be VERY helpful. So don't rule them out as an option for someone.

I'm Not Careless

January 21, 2013 at 11:50 AM

I can't seem to keep up with my bills, but why do people think it's because I'm carelessly spending my money? Is it really careless to buy a $70 pair of good walking shoes when I tend to go through the cheap pairs every 3 months and I have a hole in my current ones? Is it really careless to spend $250 on an oil change and a replacement of a car part that died? Is it really careless to spend $20 on a DVD that I've been waiting to watch for the past 2 years and it's the first one I've bought in months? Is it really carelessly spending to buy myself a $15 new fitted bed sheet because my old one had been used so long that it had a hole in it? Is it really carelessly spending to buy myself $45 tanks of good quality gas a few times a month for my car so that it doesn't break down as often? Yes, I buy some junk food. Yes, I go out to eat once in a while. But it's because I need to have a life outside of working so hard to pay off these items. I'm not buying myself an iPad, a 42" HDTV, a sports car, a designer dress, etc. I'm buying items that allow me to live a somewhat functional life.

Social Networking

January 25, 2013 at 1:45 PM

I have family. My immediate family lives closer to me, but my extended family lives out of state. This means that I have to go on "vacation" to visit them, since it doesn't make much sense for them all to come out to visit the few of us. The problem with this situation is that, as someone with Asperger's, "vacation" and traveling stresses me out more than it helps. I REALLY want to see my family, but the stress of that traveling and lack of routine and comforting space takes away from the joy of the visit. Instead of being able to spend time with the family, I usually end up tucking myself away, having meltdown after meltdown, and being unable to deal with so many people at once. It's so bad that I haven't seen my family in about 5 years.

But the other day, I noticed something. As much as I enjoy hanging out with a few people in person, I tend to MEET people better online. I tend to interact more easily and understand people better. I have time to process what they say, without the pressure of face to face communication. If I need a break...well, I just don't respond. And now the social networks have begun to help me get close to my family again.

I understand the RULES of social networking better than I understand the rules of being social in person. Likes and shares on Facebook are nice. Favorites and retweets and mentions on Twitter are all nice. Unfollowing or unfriending are signs that someone isn't happy, and it's more complicated. Blocking is when you don't want anything to do with them. I GET this. This I UNDERSTAND. Rather than those crazy, hidden rules of social interaction in person, I have found a way to socially interact pretty well online.

And by using this method that I understand, I can now have better relationships with my family. I don't HAVE to call them and visit them to show them that I care. I can "like" their status or "favorite" their tweets. They know that I'm listening and trying to connect, and not just ignoring them! I'm just using a different way to interact.

Sensory Issues With Gloves

January 29, 2013 at 9:30 AM

Well, the other day it was pretty cold (in the low 20s or the teens, and I'm talking Fahrenheit!) and when I was at work my hand almost froze to the doorknob! Literally! It started to stick and I had to quickly pull it away so it wouldn't completely freeze! I don't like to wear gloves, but I never really noticed this fact until that day. I also never fully understood WHY I don't like to wear gloves. It's not because my hands are not cold, but it's because of sensory issues that I have which are part of the Asperger's. See, the problem is when I get hair in my face. When I wear gloves, and I go to brush the hair out of my face, then there's static, which makes my hair go right back into my face again. THIS tickles my face, which makes it ITCHY, and since I'm wearing GLOVES, I have no fingers to scratch the itch, and it's just a mess and complicated! So I stopped wearing gloves quite a few years ago. I only ever wear them when I actually need to shovel snow or something and be holding onto something REALLY cold for a long time.

But, then I met this friend on Facebook. She told me that she had this spare set of fingerless gloves. Not just the kind with a hole for each finger, but literally just a hole for the thumb and then one BIG hole for all four fingers. I realized that I'd never tried something like that before. So she sent them to me, and guess what? THEY WORK! No more static! No more itchiness! (And if I do have an itch, I have the fingers to scratch it!) But best of all, NO MORE FROZEN HANDS!

I'm not saying these gloves are PERFECT. (I still get fibers everywhere, and I still have cold fingers.) However, considering the fact that my hands are not literally freezing to things, it's a step in the right direction.

Here are some other issues with clothes that I personally have due to sensory issues:

Socks: MUST be the right height, otherwise it feels strange. They CANNOT have any uneven fuzz or seams on the inside (think of the feeling of a rock in a shoe). I usually end up getting the exact same brand and type and color, and that way if I ever lose one, it doesn't really matter. I don't even put them in pairs anymore, since they are all exactly the same.

Shirts: MUST be the right material, and the neckline must be the right style. Shirts ALWAYS have to have short sleeves. (I wear my hoodie over top if I get cold.) No lace (too itchy) unless it's on the outside ONLY. No cuffs on the arms. No button-ups (too tedious) and no zippers (too cold).

Hamster Problems

February 4, 2013 at 10:15 PM

My poor baby, Charlie, the hamster, is dealing with some issues right now. He keeps scratching at himself excessively. He will just sit in the corner of his cage, in his wheel, or in his bed and scratch with his hind legs. After looking up about this online, he could have mites. ☹ The good news is that, because I work at an animal hospital, I get free pet exams. So I will be bringing him in to see the vet in a day or so. Let's all hope that everything checks out okay.

I Don't Have Time

February 5, 2013 at 11:55 AM

I feel like everyone is yelling at me to make more time for them, but I honestly just can't. I have work, doctor's appointments, autism services, presentations and more. People start asking me "Well, do you not want to do this?" and it makes me so frustrated. It's not that I don't WANT to do these things, it's that I can't help the fact that there aren't more than 24 hours in a day. I don't want to give up ANYTHING, and the fact that people are asking me to choose makes things even more difficult. I need to make more money, I need to stay healthy, I need the autism services, and I need them ALL to make sure my life keeps moving ward. How can I choose what's best for me if what's best for me is NOT making a choice?

Analogy of A Duck

February 23, 2013 at 10:30 AM

The other day, I went to visit a teacher whom I haven't seen in over 10 years. It was wonderful to reconnect with someone who helped me through my school years. My favorite topic we discussed, however, was about the duck.

I really love ducks. I feel they truly represent me, and I never realized how much so. On the surface, they may look perfectly fine, happy, and healthy. Underneath, however, is what people forget about. How hard they may be paddling just to stay afloat, and how close they may be to sinking. I don't say this to scare people. I just say it to remind them to look at the whole picture. I may be doing well, but I work SO hard to be here.

The Meltdown Process

March 22, 2013 at 2:45 PM

What happens when I have a meltdown? All I can do is think. I think about everything that I'm struggling with. I think, "What am I going to do about it?" If I don't know, I cry/scream/comfort myself and move on to the next issue. I go through these issues one by one until I have nothing left to think about and I've let out my emotions for all of them. If I don't do this process, then I will shut down mentally. I will not think about the issues at all and I will not care about them. That's why, even while they are no fun, meltdowns are a part of my life.

Eating Habits

March 24, 2013 at 10:50 AM

I've heard so many people tell me that if I don't eat something, I'm not going to get anything else… that I don't have a choice in the matter. For me, this is exactly how it is all the time. If I don't like something, I literally won't eat it and I would rather go hungry than force myself. I do this on my own sometimes because I get in moods where I don't feel like eating anything in particular. I don't have an eating disorder, I'm just VERY picky. I WILL throw it up (body's automatic reaction, not a choice) if I eat something I don't want to. Don't tell me that if I don't eat it, I don't have to have anything. Ask me if I am hungry. If I am, help me to find a way to eat what you have cooked. It could be as simple as taking out spices or cutting up the food into smaller pieces, or even setting a plate aside for me to fix it the way I want to on my own.

<u>The Realities of Advocacy</u>

March 26, 2013 at 9:10 AM

Advocating is very hard to do. You have to have enough confidence to believe in yourself and know what you are saying is the truth. You have to care enough to help others, but you have to love yourself enough to care about helping yourself, too. You have to have a strong enough way to communicate your ideas, and you need to be consistent. Last and most important, you need to be a VERY positive thinker. There is SO much negativity in the world of advocating, and you need to have a way to keep others from bringing you down while helping to lift others up at the same time.

So why have I chosen this as one of my paths in life? I've chosen it because I want to make a difference in the world. I want to be the person I wish I had when I was younger. I want to help others and myself at the same time. When I feel as though I can't go on, the love from others helps me to remember that I have a purpose.

I will never forget the first person I helped. A child was struggling with getting their diaper changed, to the point that they were having meltdowns. The child was doing fine, but suddenly had trouble with it. I asked the parent if anything was different about the process, and they said they had changed from cloth to disposable diapers. I told them to go back to the cloth, as it probably feels better on the skin. They switched, and the meltdowns stopped. I had helped a parent to understand their child and the child to feel better.

Sure, advocating can be hard, but it's totally worth it.

What Does Awareness Mean To You?

March 28, 2013 at 10:40 AM

As the month of March comes to an end, many people in the autism community are getting excited about April. Why? Because April is officially recognized as Autism Awareness Month. Even better, April 2nd is World Autism Awareness Day. Many people are getting ready to spread awareness. However, what exactly does awareness mean?

Does awareness mean changing light bulbs to the color blue? Does it mean participating in a walk? Does awareness mean telling your family for the first time that you are on the spectrum? Maybe it just means donating time or money to your favorite cause. Yet, do these ways actually spread awareness?

Dictionaries seem to define awareness as "having the knowledge of". So how do we share this knowledge?

In my personal opinion, the best way of spreading awareness would be the third action listed above. "Telling people for the first time that you are on the spectrum". Now those people are aware that you are on the autism spectrum. Now, they are aware of autism.

There is a second question here, though. Many people in the autism community are asking for MORE than awareness. Quite a few people have said that awareness is not enough. That acceptance is more important. Yet, the way I see it, there cannot be acceptance without awareness first. For, how can one accept something that they are not even aware of yet?

This is the reason why I ask for THREE different concepts when I advocate. I try to spread the idea of awareness, acceptance, AND understanding. So, when April comes around (although, there's no reason why we can't spread these concepts all year round...) please help me to advocate.

Autism Advocacy
April 8, 2013 at 6:10 PM

I had a dream the other night. I dreamed that I was finding my way through an area that seemed very familiar, yet still confusing. There was something else amazing about this place, though. Signs. Everywhere I looked I could see signs about autism awareness, acceptance, and understanding. There was a HUGE autism event just down the street and everyone was going to it. No one was upset with me when I misunderstood something, and I felt accepted. My goal in life is to make this dream come true.

I'm finally figuring out how to ACT on these ideas. I'm looking into places to visit and asking about advocating at them. I'm trying to broaden my transportation routes. And I'm determined to DO something instead of sitting around and waiting for others to ask me. I can't WAIT to get out there.

Independence

April 20, 2013 at 11:40 AM

Most people say that college years are the best years of their lives. I never really went to college. So far, the first year living on my own has been the best year of my life (minus my dog passing away). However, it's been a struggle. I'm worried that people think I'm incapable of living independently, and will pull in the reins. Without these people, I probably wouldn't BE living independently. Because of all of this, I'm TERRIFIED that this will be the first and last year of being so independent. I know I can do it eventually, but I also can tell that no one will be patient enough to wait for me to learn my own ways in the world. Rome wasn't built in a day.

Interrupting

April 28, 2013 at 8:50 AM

I can't stand it when people interrupt me. Not only is it rude, but I have a hard enough time communicating already. I know it SEEMS like I communicate just fine, but what you DON'T see is the fact that, most of the time, I can't say the words that I want to. I will end up saying something similar but not quite what I mean, and then it gets misinterpreted. So then I just give up.

Don't get me wrong, I'm guilty of doing this, too. Trust me, after years of being reminded of my manners, I know I'm guilty! I also know that I'm not the only one.

Picky Eater

May 4, 2013 at 4:50 PM

People don't realize that when they ask me to "try new foods," they are asking me to do something awful. It's as if they are asking me to eat dirt. That's literally what it feels like to me. First, there's a taste that I'm not used to. My body instantly rejects it at first, unless it smells good to me. Then, there's the texture. Then, I have to swallow it. Then I have to deal with a leftover taste and texture in my mouth. It's SO uncomfortable, that I had a meltdown just thinking about it. I don't like being a picky eater. I wouldn't be a picky eater if my body gave me that choice. Sometimes, I get lucky and I find something new that I really enjoy. But it's SO rare. So when people tell me "eat it or starve," I feel like they are telling me "I don't care." And that hurts. Yes, I know there are people in third-world countries who don't get to eat daily. I would give them some of my own meals if I could. But for me, I honestly feel that starving is just as bad as having to eat something my body doesn't like.

Looking Back:

A month after writing this blog post, I talked with someone who works with the autism services that I receive. Then I wrote this extra post:

It's NOT Just Picky Eating!

June 4, 2013 at 9:35 AM

For the first time yesterday, someone from my autism services validated my issue with eating. They confirmed with me that I am NOT just being a picky eater. They explained that they've experienced the same issues with others on the spectrum they have worked with. They even told me that they know someone who thinks they are malnourished due to the issue. Finally. Someone who understands that it's NOT that I don't have the money. It's NOT that I don't LIKE the food. It's NOT that I'm not HUNGRY enough. It's that I literally CAN'T eat. People think "Oh well. If they don't want to eat, they don't have to eat. They will eat when their body is hungry enough for it." Those people are wrong. I have gotten to the point where I get so shaky and so light-headed that I think I will pass out. I STILL cannot eat. It's not medication. It's not that I'm picky. It's not JUST a sensory issue. It's something else. I get to a point where I can't even eat my favorite foods in the world. Apparently, this may have something to do with the autism. And apparently, it doesn't affect everyone on the spectrum, which makes it SO hard to recognize in people. I finally feel like someone has heard me about this issue and cares. Finally.

Author's note:
What I have found helps me with this issue is to get juice, milk, or a powder mix to add to a liquid. It's easier to take a small sip of something than it is to chew and swallow an entire meal.

Goldilocks and The Three Chairs

May 5, 2013 at 9:35 AM

There once lived a family who had a beautiful dining table and four chairs to go with it. Now, these chairs were covered in a decorative fabric that accented the family's home. For a long while, the fabric was nice and soft (at least, Goldilocks thought so). Over the years, it grew worn and withered. The mother decided to change the fabric.

While the change in the fabric was pretty, it was also very rough on the skin. Goldilocks was uncomfortable at first. She felt it scratching and did not enjoy the change. Eventually, she grew accustomed and felt that she could slide into the chairs.

One day, Goldilocks moved out, and when she came back to visit her family, she found the chairs once again covered in a new fabric. Thank goodness she didn't live there anymore! It wasn't that they didn't look pretty. But when she tried to sit down THIS time, the texture was so different once again. She could no longer slide into the chair. Again, the change was difficult.

The moral of the story? When Goldilocks finds the chair that is "just right," she's going to find it very difficult to change to a new one.

(Yes, I'm Goldilocks.)

Weightless

May 5, 2013 at 5:50 PM

When I was old enough to ask my Mom if I could play with the scale, my Mom got rid of it. She hasn't had one since. I'm grateful for that. I didn't grow up thinking about my weight. I grew up instead thinking about my health. I'm not worried about how "fat" I look, but how unhealthy I may feel. Am I eating enough protein? Have I been exercising enough to keep myself happy? Am I sleeping well? Have I been drinking enough water lately? Once in a while, I will look at myself, and I will think "I wonder if I'm fat." But seconds later, I realize...I don't really know what "fat" is. So I must look fine, and I need to focus on making sure I feel healthy.

Health, to me, will never be about losing weight. I have never gone to a gym to work out. I don't go on a diet to buy a swimsuit. (That being said, they need to make swimsuits a bit bigger!) If something doesn't fit, I don't wear it. I assume that half of the clothes I wear shrink from being washed, not from me getting bigger. I wear stretch jeans, and belts that tie. I don't even remember what size I am half of the time.

I don't know how much I weigh. It fluctuates. And I really don't care. As long as my body feels good, that's all that matters.

Thank you, Mom, for allowing me to grow up "weightless."

"Excuses"

May 12, 2013 at 11:40 AM

When people ask me to do something and I make up an excuse not to do it, I'm not making up the excuse because I'm being lazy (most of the time). I'm usually making up the excuse because I don't know how to explain that if I push myself to do any more at that moment, or to do what has been asked of me, I may end up in a meltdown. It may be because I'm feeling overwhelmed, or because the job you have asked me to do affects me some way. Maybe the sound of the job hurts my ears, or maybe it's visually overwhelming, or perhaps I'm not focusing well enough to accomplish the task in a reasonable amount of time. There are so many factors that go into my decision of doing something. If I was able to, I would help out everyone all of the time.

Today is Mother's Day, which makes this idea even more difficult for me. My Mom asked me if I wanted to help put down mulch in the yard. My "excuse" was that I didn't have the right clothing for the job. My Mom knew better. She didn't know WHY I didn't want to do help, but she wasn't expecting me to agree to it. I still don't know exactly why I couldn't help today. Was I thinking about the insects that would be buzzing in my ears? The feeling of the dirt or gritty gloves on my hands? Not knowing exactly how long it would take? All of these factor in. But my Mom is amazing, and she knows it. She realized that even though I couldn't help her with the yard, I DO still love her very much.

A Post For Parents

May 31, 2013 at 10:05 AM

People always tell me that I'm brave for speaking and advocating about my life on the spectrum. But you know what? I'm not really that brave. No, I think the people who are brave are the ones who listen. Most parents hear the worst from doctors. They hear things like "Your child may never speak." or "Your child may not ever be able to live independently." So after hearing such sobering news, it shouldn't surprise me that most parents don't want to hear anything about autism other than possible cures. They've been traumatized. It's like someone has told them their child is dead, they have grieved, and now someone is telling them that their child might be alive. They are tired. They can't bear to go through that grieving process again. Even if they don't have to. This post goes out to those parents and caregivers who are brave enough to continue to listen. Those who face their fears to hear the hope. The fact that there is ALWAYS a chance that their child may speak...even if it's in the child's own way. The fact that their child has a possibility to live an independent life. The fact that autism is NOT a death sentence, but just a different lifestyle. Thank you, to those parents who are brave enough to hear that.

In Conclusion

So much has changed since I started writing this book. I'm almost 25 years old. While I no longer have a job, I still enjoy volunteering and helping others. My goal is to continue this advocacy work and create more autism awareness, acceptance, and understanding. I hope that this book has helped someone to better understand Asperger's Syndrome.

Lastly, let me leave you with something to think about. I always had trouble explaining to people why I had such a difficult time understanding things that seemed to come so easy for others. So I decided to write this little essay that expressed what it is like for someone like me on the spectrum. It was one of the first times that I think I was able to get my point across, and I often refer back to this example.

Asperger's Example

Take a Sherlock Holmes mystery. Imagine there are 10 paragraphs, each one of equal value of information to solve the mystery. Neurotypical people have the entire story. They can read it all. They may not understand a word or two, but they have the rest of the context to help them figure it out. People with Asperger's only get maybe 2 or 3 of these paragraphs, and aren't able to figure out the words they don't know. But they still have to solve the mystery. Sure, they may be able to figure it out, with a few good guesses and a lot of hard thinking. However, it's hard to expect that they would be able to solve the mystery. In fact, they may even get a quick (and I mean *quick*) glimpse of the whole story, but not enough for them to remember it all. They are lucky to learn one or two extra clues. When they come across a word they don't know, they lose the idea that word brings to the sentence.

Imagine living life like this every day, maybe even multiple times a day. And the people with the whole story have no idea that you missed out on a lot of information, and think you are so stupid to not be able to solve it. They see you as someone who is lazy and doesn't want to work to try to figure out the mystery, when in reality, you can't work any harder than you already are. It comes very easily to them, and they take that for granted.

CPSIA information can be obtained
at www.ICGtesting.com
Printed in the USA
FSHW012021181118
53883FS